VIA FOLIOS 90

Waiting for Yesterday

Pages from a Street Kid's Life

Michael Parenti

BORDIGHERA PRESS

Library of Congress Control Number: 2013932359

Cover illustration by Jennifer Brouse

Printed in the United States.

Published by
BORDIGHERA PRESS
John D. Calandra Italian American Institute
25 West 43rd Street, 17th Floor
New York, NY 10036

VIA FOLIOS 90
ISBN 978-1-59954-058-0

DEDICATIONS

This book is dedicated to the memory of some special friends who have left this world—but not entirely: Philip Meranto, Robert Campus, Will Miller, Michael Maggio, Joseph Papaleo, Frank Feminella, Tony Cordella, and Bill Sorrentino.

ACKNOWLEDGMENTS

My thanks to Thomas Fararo, Howard Kahn, Jack Assainte, Michael Calabrese, Angel Ewing, Carlo Ferretti, and my son Christian Parenti for their assistance and encouragement. A very special thanks goes to Jenny Tayloe who urged me onward from the very beginning and who convinced me that I had engaging stories to tell. A word of appreciation also to my editor at Bordighera Press, Anthony Tamburri, who showed much patience and good judgment through-out, and to Lisa Cicchetti who helped wrap it all up.

TABLE OF CONTENTS

Waiting for Yesterday

1/ Dear Reader (Yes, I'm Talking To *You*)

No names have been changed to protect the innocent. There are no innocents in this book. Some names have been changed to protect the author.

Herein you will find vignettes of my working-class neighborhood, family, school, religion, and Italian-American ethnic identity, and many of the people who gave life to it all. I entitle this endeavor *Waiting for Yesterday* because even though yesterday has already been lived, we often seek to revisit it with fresh understanding. We rummage through a mute past hoping to extract fragments of experience and feelings that we can weave together in an engaging and meaningful way.

Within these pages I offer personal reflections, sometimes as the critical observer and other times as the active participant. I also discuss larger issues, including the immigrant ambivalence toward American life, our society's ethnic stereotypes, the seemingly indelible mafia stigma, and even a discussion of Italy's performances in both World Wars.

One's personal early-life experiences often turn out to have significance and interest for people of diverse social backgrounds. What we are drawn to in another's life is both the novelties and the recognitions.

This is a wide ranging personal memoir seasoned with commentary about broader social realities, including how the forces of culture, class, and ethnicity act upon our lives as we come of age. The hope is that the reader is treated to an enjoyable and informative read, one that applies not only to the Italian-American experience but to the human comedy in general. *Buon appetito!*

~ Part 1: The Family ~

2/ I Am Born Under Perilous Circumstances

It was in New York City, way back in 1933, when I made a fit-ful entrance into the world. It was in "the olden days" before tele-vision or jet planes or six-lane highways or wide screen movies or cell phones. It was in the depths of the Great Depression. My birth was a cesarean because, as my mother later asserted: "You didn't want to come out. You were stubborn even then." The real story is something else.

Since Mamma suffered from a serious congenital heart dis-ease, there was some question as to whether both of us would survive the blessed event. The delivery promised to be an espe-cially difficult one. In those days during a dangerous birth, a doc-tor might crush the baby's head in order to remove it piece by piece from the womb. This was done to avoid an injurious—and possibly fatal—blockage or ripping inside the mother.

The Catholic Church strenuously opposed this grisly proce-dure. The Church's position was to let nature take its course and make no deliberate sacrifice of one life to save the other. This meant that sometimes the baby came out alive but the mother died, or sometimes both perished.

At one point the doctors asked my father for written permis-sion to have my life sacrificed were it to prove necessary to save his wife. Obeying his heart instead of the Church, my father readi-ly agreed. As it turned out, they decided on a last minute cesarean section, a risky operation in 1933 for a woman with an enlarged heart condition. "Untimely ripped from his mother's womb." I was so struck by those words from *Macbeth* when I read Shakespeare years later. Happily none of the ripping proved fatal. Both of us survived the ordeal. So did my father.

I was a cheery, healthy, easy-going baby never sick a day until the age of three. At three, however, I got a slight inflammation in my throat. My mother took me to a doctor who did what most doctors of that day did. He put me in a hospital and subjected me to a tonsillectomy.

After my tonsils were carved out of my throat, I turned into a sickly kid, catching mumps, diphtheria, influenza, German measles, whooping cough, chicken pox, and one or two other afflictions in rapid succession. This, my parents told me many times. They would remark with puzzlement: "You were never sick, then once you had your tonsils taken out, you caught every disease in the book." They had no idea what to make of it.

In those days and for years afterward, almost everyone had their tonsils removed, being urged to do so by their doctors. It was all the medical fashion much as gall bladder removals are the de rigueur procedures of today. We now know that many if not almost all tonsillectomies are unnecessary. We also now think that tonsils play a supporting role in one's immune system. I wish I still had my tonsils. You might say I miss my tonsils. No joke, I have been plagued since childhood with adenoidal irritations despite the tonsillectomy—or, perhaps, because of it.

Another surgical affliction delivered upon (male) children by knife-happy doctors was, and still is, circumcision. At the time of my birth, circumcision was becoming all the rage and has since developed into a multi-million dollar industry. For generations in America, at one time or another, circumcision has been promoted as a curative for bedwetting, masturbation, tuberculosis, asthma, epilepsy, and more recently even as a preventive against syphilis, herpes, cervical cancer, HIV and AIDS. I'm not making this up.

Circumcision is often cheerily described by its proponents as "snipping off the foreskin," as if one were dealing with a hanging cuticle. A majority of newborn males in the United States are subjected to this involuntary and sometimes harmful procedure. The infants have no choice in the matter. The foreskin, a mobile sheath with thousands of nerve endings, is torn back and sliced off the penis shaft, causing loss of blood, severe pain, and a hurtful healing period. Of the million or more infants circumcised every year in the USA, some few hundreds have their penises slashed, disfigured, or even rendered dysfunctional. In rare instances death has resulted.

So one of the perilous circumstances of my birth was circumcision. It hovered over my crib ready to strike. Fortunately for me, my untutored but sensible working-class parents would not allow the doctors to carve their way into my aspiring appendage. I was not circumcised. I left New York Hospital and went home to East Harlem intact.

When taking stock of things that have happened in your life, sometimes it is also worth taking stock of things that have *not* happened.

ಬ

3/ When Haarlem *Became Harlem*

For readers unacquainted with the history of New York City: In 1609 the Dutch established a colony on the island of Manhattan, naming it New Amsterdam, which served as the capital of a wider area called New Netherlands. Haarlem was a Dutch village in upper Manhattan, formally organized in 1658.

Along came the British in 1664 to steal Haarlem and all of New Netherlands from the Dutch. I could never feel too sorry for the Dutch, given that they had stolen those same lands from Native Americans ("Indians"), specifically the Iroquois and Algonquian. As you might have heard by now, the British changed the colony's name from New Amsterdam to New York. For decades afterward, however, Harlem was still spelled *Haarlem*, in keeping with the Dutch addiction to double vowels.

What about *East* Harlem, the hallowed ground of my childhood? East Harlem is the area reaching roughly from Fifth Avenue across to the East River and down to Yorkville. Its northern boundary was the Harlem River, which connected to the East River.

West of Fifth Avenue, stretching north and northwest was the famous African-American neighborhood of Harlem proper. It has a more diverse population these days as large numbers of Whites, Latinos, Asians, and others have moved in.

~ Leftover Scraps of History ~

The original Haarlem still exists, of course. It is a city in the Netherlands located on the river Spaarne, twelve miles west of Amsterdam. To this day within New York's (Black) Harlem there is a major street named Amsterdam Avenue; the name is a historical fossil dating back to Dutch colonial rule of New Amsterdam.

On 116th Street in the heart of Italian Harlem there was a settlement house that provided after-school activities for us neighborhood kids. It was named Haarlem House, still spelled the Dutch way 280 years after the Dutch had departed, a nice touch and another historical fossil.

For at least the last two centuries East Harlem has been what sociologists call a *first settlement area* for immigrant newcomers, the place they go to live after arriving here from *the other side* (meaning the other side of the Atlantic Ocean). In East Harlem these included Germans, then Irish, Scandinavians and Finns; then Jews, Italians and Puerto Ricans.

From the 1890s to the late 1950s East Harlem was predominantly Italian. Indeed the area has been referred to as "Italian Harlem" by residents, community leaders, and worthy writers like Gerald Meyer, Robert Orsi, and Jonathan Gill. Farther south, below 106th Street and westward was mostly Puerto Rican or what came to be known as "Spanish Harlem" or *El Barrio* as the Puerto Ricans called it. In recent years, Central American Latinos, Haitians, and others have been moving into all parts of East Harlem.

The Italian Harlem of my youth consisted of a congestion of tenements and brownstones wherein resided the largest Italo-American community in the United States, numbering over 90,000 souls. The backyards were a forest of clotheslines, poles, and fences. The cellars, with their rickety wooden steps and wrought iron banisters, opened directly onto the sidewalks. On warm days the streets were a focus of lively activity, with people coming and going or lounging on stoops and chatting. Small groups of men engaged in animated conversations, while children played ball in the streets or raced about wildly.

On certain days horse drawn carts offered a lush variety of fruits and vegetables trucked in from Jersey and Long Island farms. The cries of the vendors were of a Southern Italian cadence unspoiled by a half-century in the new land. Women sat at windowsills with elbows planted on pillows, occasionally calling down to acquaintances or yelling at the children. There was always something of interest going on in the streets, but rarely anything of special importance except life itself.

ॐ

4/ *Grandma Maria, Magic Healer*

No ethnic memoir would be complete without some mention of one's immigrant grandparents. Like most of the Italian immigrants in America, my grandparents came from the impoverished lands of the *Mezzogiorno,* or what we would call Southern Italy, bringing with them all the strengths and limitations of their people. They were frugal, hardworking, biologically fertile, and rigidly resistant to novel and venturesome ways.

The *Mezzogiorno* was impoverished because of centuries of exploitation by aristocratic rulers, Vatican landowners, and foreign occupation. The plunder from above created severe poverty and desperation below. The harshness suffered by those at the bottom had a distorting effect on their life chances and life attitudes. Survival became the prime preoccupation.

Those who exploit poor people are the first to blame the indigent for the misery imposed upon them. "If only the poor would learn to save their money." "If only the poor knew how to behave like human beings instead of animals." I have heard these and other such comments directed at indigent people in a number of locales and countries.

Regarding my own family, one of my grandmothers had thirteen children of whom seven survived. The other had fourteen with eight survivors. This was the traditional pattern of high fertility and high mortality carried over from the impoverished old country. Given the heavy burden of endless pregnancies and births, both my grandmothers died years before my grandfathers.

Their children, however, adopted the American style of smaller families. Having discovered birth control and urban living, and trying to survive the Great Depression, the second generation rarely had more than two or three offspring. The image of the large Italian family is an anachronism that hardened into a stereotype. The second and third generations in America chose fewer children, as has been the case in Italy itself since about the 1950s.

My father's mother, Grandma Maria, was a living prototype of her generation: a short squat woman who toiled endlessly in the home. She shared the common lot of Italian peasant women: cooking, cleaning, and tending to the family, with a fatalistic submergence of self. *"Che pu' fare?"* ("What can you do?") was the common expression of the elderly women. Given their domestic confinement, they learned but a few words of English even after decades of living in New York.

The immigrant women accepted suffering as a daily experience, rather than as something extraordinary. They suffered while mending and washing clothes in their kitchens, or standing over hot stoves. They suffered through their perpetual pregnancies. They suffered while climbing tenement stairs, or tending to the children or sitting alone at their windows. And they suffered while praying to their saints and burying their dead. Many of them went through life dressed in black, in an uninterrupted state of mourning for one or another kin.

Maria often cast her eyes up toward the kitchen ceiling and muttered supplications to Saint Anthony of the Light Fixture. She lived in fear of *u malocchio*, the evil eye. When younger members of the family fell ill, it was because someone had given them *u malocchio*.

Save us from our neighborhood adversaries and their vile spirits, O saints in heaven! Maria suspected the evil eye came from one or another wicked personage who bore a grudge for some forgotten reason. There were so many potential enemies in the village of New York, maybe even worse than in Italy.

Like a high priestess, Grandma Maria would sit by my sickbed and drive away the evil eye, making signs of the cross on my forehead, mixing oil and water in a small dish and uttering incantations that were a combination of witchcraft and Catholicism. Witchcraft was once the people's religion, having been in Southern Italy many centuries before Catholicism and having never quite left. Maria's magic measures seemed to work, for sooner or later I always recovered.

Grandma Maria had another healing technique. There were times when as a very young child I might fall and hurt myself. If she was present I would run crying to her and she would hold me, rub the bruise gently but with a certain feigned urgency and vigor, all the while showing sympathetic signs of pain herself: *"ooh meh neen, ooh meh neen"*[1] *"oooh, povero figgyu [figlio] meh"* (oh, poor child of mine). She would wail and moan along with me, her face contorted, suffering flawlessly as if she were absorbing my pain, making it her own.

~ *U Malocchio* on Television ~

Some of the first-generation Italians were extreme in their preoccupation with the evil eye. I remember as late as the 1950s, in New York City, a few of the late arriving postwar immigrants (from small isolated villages in Southern Italy) would put an open pair of scissors, with one blade deliberately broken off halfway, on top of the television set so that no one appearing on the TV screen could send *u malocchio* into their homes. As we now know, the baneful effects of television are not warded off that easily.

The performance always seemed to lessen my hurt both because of her intense empathy and also because it so distracted me from my own complaint. Who knows? Maybe in some way she actually was absorbing some of the pain. In any case, it was a welcomed relief and I always came away somewhat impressed by her rendition.

ชช

5/Grandma Concetta, Midwife Healer

My mother's mother, Grandma Concetta, was something of an exception to the portrait of the Italian immigrant woman I just sketched. Endowed with a strong personality and a vital intelligence, she turned to one of the few respectable professions open to rural Southern Italian women in the late nineteenth century: she

---

[1] A dialect rendition of "O *mi nino, o mi nino*"(oh my little one).

9

became a midwife, a skill she learned in Calabria and brought with her to East Harlem.

In those days midwives did more than deliver babies. They advised families on the care of children, diagnosed and treated illnesses with herbs, dietary regimens, heat applications, and other natural remedies that were said to work with far less destruction and sometimes more efficacy than the expensive chemicalized drugs pushed by the profit-driven medical and pharmaceutical industries of today.

Grandma Concetta had a great store of treatments for various ailments. My father, who always spoke highly of his mother-in-law and seemed to have more affection for her than for his own parents, once mentioned that she "would give you something for a headache and it would make your pain go away better than anything you could get from the drugstore today."

Much of the Italian folk medicine was forever lost as these immigrant midwives died off. They had no organized commercial network that could sustain and market their remedies as do, say, Chinese herbalists and acupuncturists of today. If anything, midwife practices were probably illegal by the 1920s if not earlier. Heedless of the outside world, Concetta worked solo in the neighborhood. Her five daughters (and two sons), the Di Lorenzo family, had no interest in learning her secrets and skills, no thought of maintaining the practice of an old-fashioned immigrant midwife. Instead they took the modern route, visiting whatever doctors and clinics that were affordable.

Working long hours and bearing many children, Concetta died at the age of sixty, a few years before I was born. I knew her only from the testimony of others and from a few faded photographs of a woman who gazed into the camera with a gentle strength and self-assurance.

Speaking of photographs, years ago I had in my possession an album of old family pictures including one of my maternal grandmother and grandfather, looking very young but very Old World, taken in about 1885 while they were still in Italy. Grandma Concetta Di Lorenzo, the midwife, was dressed in a rough-hewn peasant skirt and blouse, as from a different century. The bulky skirt draped down to her shoes. Next to her was my maternal grandfather, sitting stiffly in a cast-iron black suit, holding a cane in his hand with authoritative effect. The picture was a sepia masterpiece whose faded tint did honor to spirits long gone.

Unfortunately when I was a foolish youth in my late twenties, I gave momentary credence to a liberatory notion propagated by some self-appointed inspirationalists, the forerunners of latter-day New Age gurus. Their feel-good sunshine message was: "We make our own reality and our own happiness; we must not be imprisoned by the past but must make a clean break from it; we must live fully, thrusting ourselves ever forward into the here and now, putting the past behind us," etc. etc.

Acting on this blather, I impulsively tossed that trove of priceless photos into the trashcan as a step toward liberating myself from a "dead" yesterday. Some weeks afterward I realized what a damnable foolish thing I had done. I had amputated a part of my own history, dear family ghosts fixed in faded time, peering at me across the centuries. To this day, I cannot think about the loss of those family photographs without regret.

℘

6/ Grandma Doesn't Always Have to be Italian

Not long ago, I chanced upon an Internet commentary about health care. It contained an entry by an African-American man from Detroit named Elder Edwards, whom I quote in full: "Many of our grandparents' home remedies worked better than today's medicine." Here was an unequivocal corroboration of my opinion regarding folk medicine—from someone from another ethnic group.

Speaking of that other ethnic group, in 1975 I was a guest faculty member in the political science department at Cornell University. One day I was having lunch with a professor in the Black Studies program. Somehow we got onto the subject of our respective grandmothers.

His African-American grandma was a farm woman from the impoverished South who had very little schooling and who lived her later years in a Northern urban working-class environment. My Grandma Maria Parenti was an impoverished peasant woman from Southern Italy, illiterate, who lived her later years in a Northern urban working-class environment.

His grandma would bake hot biscuits and yams, boil grits and fry mounds of sausages, and other such sinfully delicious things. For the big Sunday dinners, my grandma would be up at dawn hand-making the ravioli, getting the *insalata* together, rolling and frying the meatballs, and stewing and crisping the *braciole* (flattened pieces of tender meat padded with spices then rolled up tightly).

His grandma would rule the kitchen with a firm hand, taking the rolling pin to any bothersome child who ventured in to filch one of the tasty items. My grandma would use the long wooden spoon to whack any of us who dipped a finger into the soft spicy ricotta cheese she had whipped for the ravioli (although occasionally a spoonful could be negotiated if she had some to spare).

While toiling in the kitchen my grandma would hum a little ballad, filled with sing-song Italian sentimentalities. While toiling in the kitchen his African-American grandma would hum a gospel tune.

At one point, he said, "Hey, are you sure we didn't have the same grandmother?" We shared a smile. Such a pleasantly wise joke, I thought. The hidden similarities that bind us are of greater essence than the highly visible superficial differences that so command our attention and divide us. In many instances — give or take some variations in language, artifacts, menu, and costume—the underlying script of the human comedy is very much the same. Too bad we cannot readily live with that awareness, finding reassurance in our similarities and enjoyment in our differences.

ॐ

7/ *The Old Men*

Along with the women, the immigrant men of my grandfathers' generation had toiled like beasts of burden in the old country, trapped in a grinding poverty, victimized by landlords, tax collectors, and military press gangs. Having fled to the crowded tenements of New York, they found they had a little more to live on but sometimes less to live for. My mother's father, Vincenzo Di Lorenzo, came to the United States from Calabria in 1887. He spent his working days in East Harlem carrying 100-pound bags of coal up tenement stairs, a profession that left him permanently stooped over.

My father's father, Giuseppe Parenti, arrived in 1909, a landless peasant who had worked for one of the great estates outside Bari. After his arrival in New York, Giuseppe found work, along with hundreds of other Italian immigrants, building the New York subway system. Hard and dangerous work it was, digging deep into Manhattan's mica schist and building subway tunnels under the East River. It paid $2.50 a day. Later on, for a good number of years he had an ice business, at which my father toiled through much of his childhood and early adulthood.

The Italian immigrant laborers were the paragons of the humble, thrifty toilers whom some people like to point to when lecturing the poor on how to suffer in silence and survive on almost nothing. But the immigrants were not always that compliant. If anything, they had taken the extraordinary measure of uprooting themselves from their homelands in order to escape the dreadful oppression of the Old World. Rather than suffer in silence, they had voted with their feet.

We may think of them as the virtuous poor (although in their day they were denounced as the "swarthy hordes" and the "criminal element"), but they saw themselves as lifelong victims who were somewhat less victimized in the new land than in the old. Now they worked only ten or twelve hours a day instead of fourteen and were somewhat better able to feed their children.

Still, in their hearts, many of the first-generation men nursed a sentimental attachment to Italy. As the years wore on, the old country for them became Paradise Lost while the new land often seemed heartless, money-driven, and filled with the kind of lures and corruption that distanced children from their parents. They felt little patriotic devotion to America. What kept the great majority of them in the United States were the loaves and fishes, not the stars and stripes. And keep in mind that of the millions who migrated to America, thousands returned to Italy, finding life on the other side to be more manageable.

The immigrant men drank wine made in their own cellars, and smoked those deliciously sweet and strong Italian stogies—to which I became temporarily addicted in my adulthood. We nasty youngsters called the stogies "guinea stinkers" in reference to the old Italians who smoked them.

The old men congregated in neighborhood clubs, barber shops, and the backrooms of stores to play cards, drink, and converse. They exercised an authoritative but somewhat distant presence in the home, leaving most domestic affairs including the toil of child rearing to the women.

Religion was also left mostly to the women. The immigrant males might feel some sort of attachment to the saints and the church but relatively few attended mass regularly and some openly disliked the priests. In the literal sense of the word, they were "anticlerical," suspicious of clergymen who did not work for a living but who lived off other people's labor and—as Grandpa Giuseppe Parenti said to me—did not marry but spent all their time around the women and the children in church.

The immigrant men uttered a whole litany of curses, including ones that began with the Southern Italian slang word: *mannaggia* (pronounced "mah-NAH-ja") meaning "damn it" or "curse it." So one would shout, *Mannaggia la miseria*! (Curse the misery!). Then there was *Mannaggia a chi t'è morte!* (Damn the dead!), a harsh and almost sacrilegious utterance for it referred to the deceased in one's own family. I can recall, when I was about 35-years-old, exclaiming "*Mannaggia a chi t'è morte!*" only to have my father frown and tell me to watch what I was saying. In effect, I was bringing down curses upon all the departed in our family, including his mother and mine. I hadn't even thought of its traditional application and had used the expression merely to vent a general annoyance.

In the Southern Italian culture exported to New York, from about 1870 to 1940, reverence for the dead was a serious matter. You were far more likely to be esteemed and respected if dead than if alive. As one of the deceased you had a far greater chance of having your picture placed on the mantelpiece aside a candle or a flower. Your relatives would reverentially soften their voice if your name came up in conversation. "May he rest in peace" was the accompanying incantation, along with a momentarily sad facial expression. Given all this, *mannaggia* was not the word to be enlisted against those who had traversed the great divide and presumably were closer to God than the rest of us.

One curse uttered by the old men that I found most interesting was *Mannaggia l'America*! (Damn America!). This was obviously an expression that came into vogue only *after* they had arrived in New York. Rather than gushing with gratitude for the much celebrated blessings of the American Dream, they vented their anger about the hard life imposed upon them as impoverished newcomers in the new land.

Not all of them. There were some who, if pressed on the matter, would say that their life had been tough in America but still much better than it had been in Italy—which is why they migrated in the first place, seeking an existence that was not shrouded in unremitting deprivation. I doubt that many Italian immigrants actually knew what the American Dream in all its rapturous adornments was supposed to be. Most just wanted a somewhat better life than the grinding poverty from which they had fled.

Others, like my Grandpa Giuseppe, often voiced their longing for "l'Italia, l'Italia." Grandpa never felt completely at home in America and palpably longed for the old country. I once asked him, "Grandpa, if you miss Italy so much, why did you come to America?" And he answered, "I didn't want to die in Tripoli," a response that took me awhile to decipher. It turns out that the Italian constitutional monarchy was sending press gangs around the countryside to conscript farm boys like Giuseppe into the army in order to engage in the conquest of Libya (many years before Mussolini launched his attacks upon Africa), a campaign that eventually brought on the death of half of Libya's population.

So my paternal grandfather had fled to America to avoid military conscription. Grandpa was a draft dodger not because of any principled ideological stance but simply out of a desire to avoid getting killed for no good reason by strangers in a strange land.

∞

8/ Grandfather Captivity

I have a fond memory of my maternal grandfather, Vincenzo, a stooped, toothless, unimposing old man who was my closest ally in early life. In his last few years, his mental capacity began to wilt, causing him to be relegated to the edge of the adult world in "second childhood," or what Italians call *rimbambito* (senile).

Consequently, he entered wholeheartedly into my world, playing cards with me, taking me for walks around the block, watching with undisguised delight as I acted out my highly dramatized cowboy and Indian games. He always took my side and, despite his physical and mental infirmity, was sometimes able to rescue me from the discipline of my parents—which is the God-given function of grandparents.

~ A Possible Patricide ~

My mother lived in fear that I might one day miss a bowel movement. Regularity in defecation was one of the great obsessions of her entire generation. So on occasion she fed me milk of magnesia. In those days it was the most chalky, gagging drink—unendurable. One time she handed me a large glass of that hateful liquid laxative and left the kitchen. She wanted "to see it finished" by the time she returned. In desperation I offered the milk of magnesia to her somewhat demented father, Grandpa Vincenzo, who was sitting in his rocking chair. He readily accepted it and downed the whole drink with a big smile, smacking his lips, quite pleased with himself.

Mamma returned to the kitchen, surprised to see the glass sitting on the table entirely emptied. I sat there motionless as she eyed me suspiciously. That probably was the most daring feat of deception I ever perpetrated against her, certainly at the age of five. What effect that enormous laxative drink had on my frail demented Grandpa, I cannot say. He did die not long afterward but I like to think there was no direct causality.[2]

Years before, when Vincenzo was still a youngster in his late seventies and already a widower, he was discovered to have a girl friend, a woman of about fifty years. She would steal into the house when no one was home and climb into bed with him. When

---

[2] I wrote a short story about this and other incidents relating to my maternal grandfather, including his death and funeral. It was entitled "Bereavement," published in the *Antioch Review*, v. 32, no. 4, 1973.)

family members discovered this tryst, they were utterly scandalized. In those days the idea that elderly parents might have sexual desires incited a furious embarrassment among their children. My relatives denounced the woman as a *puttan'*, a whore of the worse sort, whose intent was to drive Grandpa to an early grave by overexerting his heart.

Actually, he died at age 87, which in those days was considered an enviable accomplishment (and still today is a pretty good run). The poor lonely woman was not allowed to see Vincenzo anymore. And dear grandpa, after being scolded like a child, was kept under a sort of house arrest.

After passing a certain age, Italian grandfathers were frequently made captives by their sons, daughters, older nieces and nephews, all competing to put the old man under their protective custody. If a car came too close for comfort while grandpa was crossing the street, as might happen to any pedestrian, the family would try to keep him from taking unaccompanied strolls, convinced that he could no longer judge traffic.

If he misplaced his hat or scarf, as might anyone, he would be deemed unable to care for his personal effects. At the beach, if an Italian grandfather waded into the water much above his knees, one or another of his self-appointed guardians could be seen jumping up and down on the shore, waving frantically at him and shouting: "Oooooo, ooooo, Poppa's gonna drown! Somebody get him!" I read somewhere that this phenomenon of grandfather captivity still exists in parts of Italy.

I saw the protective custody game repeated with my paternal grandfather, Giuseppe, who in his later years presided in silence at the head of the table during holiday meals, a titular chieftain whose power had slipped away to his sons and sons-in-law who now earned the money and commanded their own households. While a certain deference was still paid him because of his age and patriarchal status, more often he found himself, much to his annoyance, a victim of overprotection. As we know, overprotection is a sure sign of powerlessness.

Years later in 1956, I had occasion to have a few long talks with Grandpa Giuseppe Parenti and discovered that he was an intelligent engaging man—although he did have a number of opinions that were strange for that time, namely that canned foods were of little nutritional value as compared to fresh foods, physical exertion was better than sitting around doing nothing, and country air was better for one's health than city air. (People concerned about air quality in those days were derisively dismissed as "fresh air fiends.") Giuseppe also believed that doctors and hospitals could be dangerous to one's survival, automobiles were the ruination of cities, and too much emphasis was placed on money and material things. We treated such views as quaintly old-fashioned.

One day he extended his left arm, slapped it hard with his right hand and said to me, "Garlic isa good fuh you. It cleansa you' blood." I could barely suppress a smile. Garlic cleans your blood? Uh, sure Grandpa, if you insist. I thought the old guy was getting a bit silly in his quaint folksy way. Still, it was a remark that stayed with me.

About two decades later, well after Grandpa's demise, I was reading an article in a nutritional health magazine regarding the beneficial effects of various fresh foods and herbs. One comment leaped from the page, leaving me wide-eyed: "Nutritional experts are finding that garlic is an effective blood cleanser."

Grandpa was so ahead of his time.

ⅎ

9/Discovering Italy in America

Many of the Italians who journeyed to America in what was known as the Late Migration of 1870 to 1930 or so did not think of themselves as Italians. Most of them were *meridionali*, denizens of the impoverished villages of Southern Italy. This included both my grandfathers. To them, the nation-state of Italy was a distant nemesis, another unwelcome layer of government and taxes contrived by the Piedmontese and other northerners.

Italy did not finalize its *Risorgimento,* its unification, until the 1860s. But this development did not readily sink into the prevailing consciousness of remote villages where the dominant mentality was locked into conformity, parochialism, and territoriality. The villagers continued to identify with their particular provinces and dialects, as they had always done. When they arrived in New York they still considered themselves to be not Italian but *napoletano, siciliano, calabrese, barese, genovese, abruzzese,* and the like.

~ The Iceman Becometh ~

Provincial origins sometimes even determined career choices. A good example was the predominance of Italians from Bari in the ice business, of which my Barese paternal grandfather was one. The Federal Writers Project produced a Depression era study entitled *The Italians of New York,* which noted that New York icemen were almost all Barese, an unusual feature since the profession of iceman was completely unknown in Bari. No mystery to this. Early in the century some of the very first Barese to arrive in New York became icemen because there was a living to be made. And when relatives and other paesani came to New York, they connected with their family predecessors and went into the same business. Armed with this information, I once smilingly asked my father, "How come all the icemen in New York have been Barese?" "Aw," he said almost defensively, "That's not true. A few of them are Sicilian."

Arriving in East Harlem, they tended to settle in distinct neighborhood enclaves. So a cluster of Barese lived around 112th Street and a mini-neighborhood of Neapolitans might be found on 115th Street, and so on, a patchquilt of provincial self-segregation. One's *paesani* were not fellow Italians but persons from the same region of Italy, a fellow Neapolitan or Sicilian or Genovese, or whatever.

These regional differences did not carry over to the Americanized offspring of the immigrants. I do not recall the provincial origins of any of my young school friends. We boys would misuse *paesan'* to mean any Italian. Having said that, I still can recall that second- and third- generation Italians who upon meeting might begin to refer to their common ethnicity and then frequently will ask each other, "What part of Italy is your family from?"

The generational difference in consciousness was brought home to me when I was almost forty years old. My father was telling me about someone who was starting a small business. I wondered if the person in question was Italian. So I asked Poppa, "Is he a *paesan'*?" and he responded, "No, he's *napolitan'*" — meaning that he was not Barese; he was from Naples or its environs. Poppa still thought (correctly) of *paesan'* not as a nationality but as referring to someone who came from the same province in the old country. I was using *paesan'* in the second-generation manner to mean any fellow Italian.

The dominant American society of course made no such provincial distinctions. To the star-spangled yahoos, a wop was a wop regardless of his provincial roots or dialect. With bigotry so generously applied to include all the various provincials, the immigrants and their children began to see themselves as did the American society, a great solid wave of Italians.

In New York the derogatory terms were democratically imposed: all Italians were "wops," and "guineas." Other terms used mostly in other regions of the USA—such as "dago" and "ghinzo" — were largely unknown in Italian Harlem.

Just as some African Americans today make defiantly friendly use of the word "nigger" when talking to and about each other, so Italians freely offered such utterances as "That crazy wop is a lot of fun" or "He's one smart guinea bastard." But were a non-Italian to use such terms, it could lead to an angry confrontation.

Like other groups before and since, the Italian immigrants were treated as unwelcome strangers, especially the impoverished uneducated *Southern* Italians. Considered incapable of becoming properly Americanized, they endured various forms of discrimination at the hands of the Anglo-Protestants, Germans, and other earlier arrivals in America (including some Northern Italians). Like other ethnic groups that have felt the sting of prejudice, many of the immigrants eventually developed a late-blooming compensatory nationalism, becoming more nationalistic regarding Italy while in the new country than when they had lived "on the other side."

Living in America, Grandpa Giuseppe, a keenly intelligent man who spoke only a Barese dialect much of his early life, listened to Italian language radio programs offered in New York including operas. Over the years he expanded his comprehension of the standard Italian language. He taught himself to read Italian by plowing through the leading Italian language daily newspaper in the United States, *il Progresso.* By the 1940s. after enough years in the new country, he became less a Barese and something of an Italian, rooting for Italy, a nation he began to identify as his very own.

So the immigrants who came here did undergo an acculturation process of sorts. While the dominant society thought of turning them into Americans, some provincials like Grandpa Parenti managed to turn themselves into Italians.

ဆာ

10/ *Why My Name Is Not Joseph*
The Italian custom was to name one's firstborn son after one's own father. Thus my great grandfather Michele (Michael) named his first-born son (my grandfather) Giuseppe (Joseph), after his

22

own father. Grandpa Giuseppe then named his firstborn son (my father) Michael, after his father of the same name. It was then assumed that I would be named Joseph to continue this endless genealogical succession of Michael-Joseph-Michael-Joseph. Not so.

It was 1928 when my parents got married. My father's parents were opposed to it. They complained that my mother was not Barese but Calabrese, "not one of us." In Italy the distance between Gravina di Puglia, the Barese hometown of my father's family and Cosenza, Calabria, the hometown of my mother's family, was not much more than 95 kilometers. The distance between the Parenti and Di Lorenzo families in New York was even closer—about five blocks. Yet they were considered worlds apart by the immigrants. One must never underestimate the provinciality of provincials.

In addition, Poppa's parents did not wish to lose their prime breadwinner. Why support an alien wife when he should be working for his own parents and siblings as he had been doing since childhood? However, my father was now coming into his own. At age 18, he gave up the horse-drawn ice wagon and taught himself to drive a battered old truck. Bucking and kicking like a horse, it was the first vehicle he ever handled. He bought it for ten dollars and converted it into one of New York's earliest motorized ice wagons.

By this time, he and his father were doing well in the ice business. They had hired a third man, and Poppa's hours were shorter. Now he had a few coins in his pocket and more time for himself. He became a snappy dresser and a superlative dancer (Waltz, Tango, Fox Trot, Charleston, Rumba), winning applause at Roseland and other dance halls that were all the rage in the 1920s. He once told me he had won the Charleston championship in Hartford, Connecticut, "though I doubt anyone would remember that," he added rather plaintively.

"I got married," my father said to me more than once, "because I was 21, holding up a big part of the family ice business, and yet I was still expected to be home by 9 o'clock in the evening." He wanted a life of his own and a woman of his own. What did he care if she was Calabrese? "Where the hell in the middle of New York City was I supposed to find a girl from the same village in Puglia?" So my parents were married, and five years later I was born, the product of a mixed-race union: Calabrese and Barese.[3]

While tradition mandated that I be named Joseph, after my paternal grandfather, my mother, having had enough of her in-laws, decided to name me Michael, in the American fashion after my own father. To clinch this maneuver she advertised the fact that St. Michael's Day was September 29 and I was born on September 30.

Among the immigrant Italians, one's birthday was nowhere as important as one's name-day (the day of one's patron saint). That I was born so closely to St. Michael's Day was ample evidence of God's intention, my mother maintained. She did not actually believe this, but the argument served an admirable Machiavellian purpose.

Years later when I started attending church, I was rather pleased to see that St. Michael was the warrior archangel. His statue—almost always a variation of Guido Reni's masterful seventeenth-century baroque painting—was of a determined figure, armed with sword, driving Satan down into the fiery pit; or the even more furiously dramatic painting not many years after Reni by Luca Giordano (*San Michele sconfigge Satana*). St. Michael was much more appealing to this street kid than most of the other saints with their delicate poses and simpering skyward gazes.

---

[3] My father's family came from Gravina di Puglia, but neither the village name of Gravina nor the provincial name of Puglia were used. Instead all the Pugliese used the name of the large city in the region, Bari, for self-identification. So they all called themselves "Barese."

Then there was the clarion call to action in the Archangel's prayer: "*St. Michael the Archangel, defend us in battle. . . O Prince of the heavenly host by the power of God thrust into hell Satan and all the evil spirits who prowl about the world seeking the ruin of souls.*" Such a furious cry stays with you for awhile.

As it turned out, my father rarely addressed me as Michael. When I was a teenager, for some strange reason he called me "Charlie." I let it go, having not the heart to tell him that Charlie was not my real name. As I grew older and more assertive in my ways, he took to calling me "boss," a title bequeathed with a tinge of irony.

In earlier years of protectiveness and concern, Poppa would revert to that strange Southern Italian custom of calling one's child by one's own family title. So a father would tenderly call his male or female child "Daddy," as when my father would say to me, "We can't go to the beach today, Daddy." A mother would call her child "Mommy," as when my mother might say to me: "Come here, Mommy, don't hurt yourself."

It carried into the fourth generation. My father called my five-year old son "Grandpa," leaving the puzzled boy to whisper to me: "Why does Grandpa call *me* 'Grandpa'?" I fumbled for an explanation: "That's just a custom. It's a way of saying you and Grandpa are close pals, or something like that."

To add further confusion: my birth certificate identifies me as Michael Parenti with no mention of my middle name, John. Most of my official documents have me as Michael John. Who the hell was John? and why do I have him as my middle name? I knew not a single relative named John. For some reason I never bothered to ask my parents about this.

My baptism certificate only further muddles things, offering a whole additional set of names. When about five weeks old, I was baptized by an Italian priest, Father Fiore, at Our Lady of Mount Carmel church in East Harlem. On the baptism certificate his Old

World script clearly has me named in Italian as Michele Giovanni Parente. So I was baptized Michele not Michael. My family name, Parente, correctly recorded both at Ellis Island and Mount Carmel church, was somehow later changed to Parenti. And crafty John sneaked in from the very beginning as Giovanni.

℘

11/ "La Famiglia, La Famiglia"

Contrary to what we may have encountered in the sentimental literature, the immigrant Italians in the New World often treated their children severely. They sent their young ones to work at an early age and expropriated their earnings. For most of the immigrant adults there was little opportunity to face the world with ease and tenderness. Of course, infants and toddlers were hugged, kissed, and loved profusely, but as the children got older it would have been an embarrassment, and in any case was not the custom, to treat them with much overt affection. Besides, there were so many of them, each new child being either an additional burden or an early tragedy but seldom an unmitigated joy.

"La famiglia, la famiglia" (pronounced "fah-MEEL-ya") was the incantation of the old Italians. The family, always the family: be loyal to it, obey it, stick with it. This intense attachment to the family was not peculiar to Italians but was, and still is, a common characteristic of almost any poor rural people—be it in the Philippines, Nigeria, India, or Appalachia. More than anything the family was one's defense against starvation and against the padrone, the landowners, magistrates, strangers, and rival families. As in any survival unit, its strictures were often severe and its loyalties intense. And betrayals were not easily forgiven.

The Italian family could also be a battleground within itself, especially among brothers and sisters who had a hard childhood ruled over by immigrant parents who themselves saw life as a series of impending catastrophes. I remember the many squabbles, grudges, and hurt feelings that passed between my father and his siblings in a series of shifting alliances and realignments.

Years later, as the siblings put the deprivations and insecurities of the immigrant family behind them and mellowed with age and post-war prosperity and the advent of children and grandchildren of their own, they tended to get along much better with each other. It was a good example of how relations within the larger society influence personal relations.

I enjoyed the nourishing embrace of the big family gatherings, the outings at the beach, the picnics, parties and holiday dinners. The Italian holiday feast was a celebration of abundance with its endless platters of tasty well-seasoned foods. I wonder if those marathon meals were a kind of ritual performed by people who had lived too long in the shadows of want and hunger, a way of telling themselves that at least on certain days the good life was theirs. Whether or not there was any larger meaning to them, the dinners were enthusiastically enjoyed.

Ethnic groups in America often learn to live in two worlds, the American world and their own (or with African-Americans it might be called the Black world and the White). After a generation or so of acculturation, more and more of the marginalized ethnic world is replaced by the standardized American one. Living in both these worlds at the same time, we switch from one to the other rather automatically. In an article I wrote decades ago I called this "cultural ambidexterity" and "dual identity."

In my family, this ambidexterity was manifested in, among other things, holiday dinners. Someone might sing an Italian song around the table, then an American one. At Thanksgiving, we began the meal with richly adorned platters of antipasto, followed by steaming plates of pasta in rich tomato sauce, along with well spiced *braciola*, meatballs, and sausages cooked to tender perfection, accompanied by huge bowls of green salads, a sumptuous Southern Italian holiday meal.

But then, after all this, out came the traditional American Thanksgiving or Christmas meal, a roasted turkey with sweet potatoes, cranberry sauce, and vegetables. The cultural conflict was overcome by piling the two different cultures onto the same table—causing groans from those who, despite their complaints about too much food, gorged themselves to a hurtful level.

~ More Ambidexterity ~

The conflicting modes of behavior demanded by two different cultures sometimes could be neatly juxtaposed and acted out simultaneously. Thus, as a child, entering a room full of people at a family gathering, I would kiss some of the men but only shake hands with some of the others. Years later, when reflecting upon such incidents, I recalled that the ones I kissed were invariably the older Italian males: my grandfather and various great-uncles such as Zi Torino and Zi Pietro, while the handshakes were reserved for the younger, more Americanized men of the family. I had learned almost intuitively, perhaps by subtle cues from the individuals involved, that to kiss an elderly Italian man was a sign of affection and respect while the same act with an American male would be sissy stuff.

Whatever the cultural contradictions, it was my good fortune to occupy a special place in two large regiments of relatives (the Parenti and Di Lorenzo families), They all seemed to treat me with special regard and appreciation—especially my numerous aunts and cousins. At family gatherings I would sometimes hold forth with one-man skits and parodies drawn from radio shows or movies or from our own family life. I would do an impersonation of Uncle Larry that caused everyone to laugh heartily, except maybe Uncle Larry. In any case, my extended family was a well-populated haven in a heartless world. In this respect I was most fortunate, perhaps much more than I realized at the time.

~ *Part Two: Community and Friends* ~

12/ "What's a Slum?"

When I was about thirteen-years-old I chanced upon an article in Henry Luce's *Life* magazine that described East Harlem as "a slum inhabited by beggar-poor Italians, Negroes, and Puerto Ricans," words that stung me and wedged in my memory.

"We live in a slum," I mournfully reported to my father.

"What's a slum?" he asked. He was not familiar with the term.

"It's a neighborhood where everybody is poor and the streets are all run-down and dumpy and dirty and filled with beggars."

"Shut up and show respect for your home," he replied. Note his choice of words. Poppa was not expressing pride in East Harlem as such. But situated within the neighborhood was our home, and you didn't want anything reflecting poorly upon family and home.

A bit taken aback by his response, I said nothing, convinced once more that my father was incapable of learning anything from his brilliant teenage son.

On my block, 118th Street, there was both *normal* poverty and *extreme* poverty. But the latter was not readily detectable. For years there was an iceman on the block who did a bustling business. This meant that there were families that did not have refrigerators—including my own. We made do with a window box that held a piece of ice and a bottle of milk and a few other perishables. Eventually we got a second-hand refrigerator.

Also on 118th Street was an old brownstone that served as a nursery for needy children. One day during my high-school years, I heard the famous writer Dorothy Parker being interviewed on the radio. (I was already familiar with her name if not her writing.) She was talking about giving aid to the poor children who were cared for in that very same settlement house on 118th Street. "Are they Negro children?" asked the interviewer. "No, I believe they are Italians," Dorothy Parker answered. The nursery for the needy was just across the street halfway down the block from my house. I often hung around that area, yet I had never seen impoverished children being escorted in or out of there; or I never thought anything of it if I did see any.

Italian Harlem had its block parties, family links, and numerous face-to-face acquaintances. Still it was not one big *Gemeinschaft*. It was not an urban village. Many people were unknown to each other even on the same block. I had to find out about the nursery for the needy from a radio interview with Dorothy Parker. That is almost pure *Gesellschaft*.

Contrary to the slur in *Life* magazine, I came to realize that, despite the extreme poverty, my neighborhood was inhabited not by "beggar-poor" derelicts but mostly by hardworking and usually underpaid proletarians, more-or-less sane folks who were the ordinary heroes of the urban landscape. The exact same thing can be said for the nearby African-American and Puerto Rican communities in Harlem

In Italian Harlem there could be found people who drove the trucks, taxicabs, trolleys, and buses. They manned the loading docks and the maintenance crews, and practically monopolized New York's building sites as construction workers, carpenters, bricklayers, electricians, roofers, glaziers, housepainters, and plumbers. And when they were not building structures, they were on the wrecking crews that tore them down.

Other Italian Americans put in long hours employed in candy stores, grocery stores, and five-and-dime stores, in dress shops, barber shops, butcher shops, and sweatshops; in beauty parlors, ice cream parlors, and pizza parlors; tending bakeries, barrooms, and poolrooms. They were bank clerks, janitors, dry cleaners, and laundresses. They were auto mechanics, machinists, manicurists, hospital workers, and gardeners; ditch diggers and gravediggers, milkmen and mailmen, shoemakers and homemakers, elevator operators and telephone operators, apartment guards and bank guards, night workers and day jobbers. They shined shoes at Grand Central Station right next to their Black coworkers, and on the Staten Island ferry. And they buffed the shiny lobbies of midtown office buildings.

They served as waiters and waitresses, cooks and caterers; secretaries and receptionists; garment cutters, tailors, seamstresses, and dress designers; fish vendors, vegetable vendors, peddlers, and truck farmers.

They worked in insurance offices and post offices. They built the highest skyscrapers and deepest subway tunnels, and years later their offspring cleaned the subway tracks and the streets and sidewalks of the whole city and collected the garbage, holding so many jobs in the Department of Sanitation that *shgoobadoen*[4] became a playful entry in everyone's name-calling arsenal.

These were the people who performed "the work of civilization" to borrow a phrase from the great economist Thorstein Veblen.[5] The working poor lived out their lives largely unsung and unnoticed. Wherever they toiled, it was almost always to "bring some money home for the family," that prime unit of survival.

---

[4] Phonetic spelling of an Italian dialect distortion of *scopettone*, meaning in East Harlem: "garbage man."

[5] Veblen was actually talking about the unsung unpaid work that *women* did all over the world.

Tucked away amidst the blue-collar ranks of Italian Harlem were the politicos who got out the vote in their neighborhood precincts for the Democratic Party. There were local lawyers and realtors; doctors, dentists, and morticians; professional musicians and many amateur ones, and photographers (mostly for weddings and Holy Confirmations); a few young toughs training to be professional boxers who might end up as downtown bouncers if they were lucky; some union shop stewards and union organizers, a struggling magazine illustrator, a comic book cartoonist, a sculptor, a tall lovely sixteen year-old girl who was working as a model downtown, young men attending City College and young women attending Hunter College, and a few aspiring opera students, including a lovely mezzo-soprano who performed with great charm at local events and at high mass at Holy Rosary Church. Then there was an occasional young man going off to the seminary to become a priest, or a young woman preparing to become a nun

---

~ Taking Casualties ~

When World War II came along, our working-class sons were drafted and were almost always channeled into the infantry, the military unit with the highest casualty rate by far. No surprise then that Italian Americans were reportedly the ethnic group that suffered the largest number of U.S. infantry casualties in that war. My cousin Vinny was wounded twice in the infantry, the first time at Normandy, the second time at the battle of St. Lo in France.

Another cousin, Anthony, was shot in the chest by a German sniper but he survived. His father, my Uncle Anthony, was seriously upset that his son had finished years of college and engineering school only to be put into the infantry. "They treat us like dumb guineas. We all have to go into the infantry and get killed." More than once did Uncle Anthony bitterly voice such sentiments.

In sum, *pace* Henry Luce and *Life* magazine, defamatory labels like "slum" and "beggar poor" can hide a multitude of virtues—not likely to be appreciated by Mr. Luce and his superrich cohorts.

There is the saying that "the slums are not the problem, they are the solution," meaning they are the place we dump the marginal and low performing groups. It might do well to remember that the slums are where hard-working low-income people live and out from which they venture to help keep society afloat.

℘

13/ "We Built This Country"

The Italian workers I knew, including my paternal grandfather, were fond of claiming "We Italians built this country." Indeed, the crews that constructed the New York subways and many of the city's imposing edifices were largely of Italian background. By the 1950s, well into the 1970s or more, workforces within the construction industry throughout the entire Northeast were predominantly Italian-American, as were the leaders (and most of the membership) of the construction unions.

Truth be told however, the Irish who came to America in the great migrations from the 1830s onward made the same claim about being the ones who built this country. And indeed, they served in the ranks, building the bridges, tenement houses, and earliest skyscrapers and rail lines. In New York the Irish working class started to unionize and fight back against terrible work conditions and miserable pay scales. The Italian immigrants, mostly impoverished peasants, were often used as strike breakers and scabs, sometimes unbeknownst to themselves, bringing them into conflict with the unionized Irish. The newly arriving immigrants knew only that they themselves needed work.

Years later as the Italians organized, they would fight against African-American and Latino workers who were brought in to break *their* unions. Sometimes the Italian workers would go up against the poor Anglo-Protestants trucked in from impoverished rural areas well outside New York City to serve as strikebreakers and scabs.

One man who patronized our neighborhood barbershop told me of his early experiences on the picket line confronting the destitute "strikebreakers" in those trucks. "Those people didn't know what they were getting into. All they was told is that there was jobs for them. We really hit them hard and practically killed some of them. I felt very bad about it. I felt sorry for them. They was just looking for work and trying to feed their families, just like the rest of us."

Along with the Italians and the Irish, other groups made claim to having built America: Poles, Germans, Chinese, Jews, Latinos, and the like. Today one can see Central and South American immigrants doing much of "the work of civilization."

In the 1960s I heard civil rights leaders proclaim that it was *Black* people who built this country. It was Black people who picked the cotton, dug the canals, scrubbed the floors, cooked the food, constructed the levees and the depots, unloaded the docks, farmed the lands, and worked the mines and mills. For generations they toiled as hard as anyone (if not harder), and in the end had little to show for it, given the special discrimination and underpayment they faced.

And finally we might pay homage to the Native Americans (a.k.a. "Indians") who for centuries tended this great continent in the pre-industrial era with care and without a driven need to accumulate, accumulate, accumulate—only to have their ancestral lands stolen and themselves slaughtered or reduced to peonage by the invading Europeans.

The claims made by *all* the various ethnic groups hold some truth. *Un mondo, molte storie* (One world, many histories). Together over the generations they *all* built this country. They were the 99% who provided the labor that produced the riches that the privileged few have always enjoyed. Only after enormous political struggle, does some, if any, of that wealth trickle down to those who created it.

◈

14/ The Struggle for Survival

After my birth the doctors warned my mother that with her congenital heart condition another pregnancy would be fatal. So I went through life as an only child. My mother tended to spoil me, for which she was criticized by her older sisters. More than once she mentioned how sorry she was that I had no brothers and sisters to play with, and she encouraged my playmates to come spend as much time as they wanted at our house. But I entertained no regrets about being an only child, for why would I want to share my lovely mother with some other little brat?

My father played a more distant role than my mother, as was the usual way in Italian working-class families—and in just about any other family where the division of labor is drawn along gender lines. He labored long hours for meager sums, sometimes two jobs at a time. Born in Italy, he was transported to this country at the age of five.

He did poorly in school because of the burdens the immigrant family imposes on its first-born son. When he was only ten years old, his day went something like this: up at 6 AM, work on his father's ice truck until 8 AM, then to school, then back to work from 3 PM to 7 PM to complete a thirteen-hour day. On Saturdays he worked from 6 AM to midnight, an eighteen-hour day. On Sunday he labored eight hours, from 6 AM to 2 PM "That was supposed to be a half-day," he remarked sadly to me years later.

He spent three terms in the first grade because he spoke so little English at home and was too exhausted from work to readily learn to read and write. Often overcome by fatigue, he would doze off in class. "Once when I fell asleep the teacher dumped

35

water on me, so I took the ink well out of the desk and threw it at her. That was in the third grade. So they said I was a bad kid. After that the teachers had it in for me even more."

By the time he finished fifth grade he was fourteen, old enough to drop out of school and work full time on the ice truck, with the eager approval of his immigrant parents who had no use for public school and its alien ways.

Many years later, I talked to him about his youthful days and recorded his thoughts. The things he remembered most were the long hours of toil, the humiliation of not being able to speak English, and the abuse he received from teachers. There was one bright spot, as he tells it:

> The only teacher who cared about me was Miss Booth because she saw me carry ice a few times on 110th Street and she asked, "How come you're carrying ice at your age?" I said, "I got to work. My father can't afford a man. There's seven of us at home to feed." So she saw I wasn't really a bad kid. She saw I was no good in school really on account of I had to work so hard. She would let me sleep awhile in the back of the room. Miss Booth, she even got me to wash the blackboard. Anything she wanted, I did because she showed she cared about me.

~ Padre Supremo ~

To illustrate the patriarchal mentality of my father's world I might recall the time he informed me in troubled tones that Uncle Americo, while drunk one night, had started beating his wife, Aunt Fanny (my mother's sister). Americo's son, my cousin Eddy, forcibly intervened and wrestled his father to the floor. What shocked my father was not Americo's behavior but Eddy's. "I don't care what happens," he concluded, "a son should never raise a hand to his father"—a pronouncement that left me wondering what I would have done had I been in Cousin Eddy's place.

Hovering over us was the Great Depression, a mysterious force that explained why there was never enough money, and why my father was away working all the time (or looking for work). I remember during one unusually difficult period when I was in the third grade, my mother bought a small thin steak and cooked it for me as a special treat. She sat watching intently as every morsel disappeared into my mouth. When I offered her a piece she declined, saying she wasn't hungry. Only years later did I realize with a pang that she very much would have wanted some. I should have insisted.

None of my relatives talked of "careers"; I don't think the word was in vogue among us. But everyone talked about jobs—or the fear of being without one. A high school education was considered an unusual accomplishment, and the one uncle who had graduated high school was considered something of a celebrity. He became a "male nurse."

My mother's dream was that I would someday get a high school diploma, for then all doors would be open to me. As she said, I would be able to "dress nice every day not just Sundays" and "work in an office," a fate that sounded worse than death to a lively street kid.

Toward the end of World War II the struggle for survival eased a bit. My father got steady work driving his uncle's bread truck and my mother found a job in a neighborhood dress factory, toiling at a sewing machine all day. The job, she told me repeatedly, would give her more "independence." What did she mean? Being married to my father how independent could she expect to be? Now I realize she was saying that she did not want to be dependent on my father for every penny. Aside from needing more income for the family, she wanted some earning power of her own. Mamma was an embryonic feminist.

I remember her to be a compassionate soul. The vulnerable and the weak, those in pain, in want, or in disgrace won her sympathy. I must have picked up these sentiments from her—or from her womb.

When I was about nine-years-old, she and I went to see the movie *Gone With the Wind*. The opening scenes showed how sweet life was for the wealthy and privileged plantation Whites. After initial frolicking, all the young ladies reclined in a large room on cots and sofas to nap away the hot afternoon and rest up for evening festivities. To ensure that they dozed in cool comfort, Black female slaves stood among them through the afternoon hours, laboriously waving large fans.

My mother and I both found the scene distasteful. "They sure are served hand and foot," she remarked disapprovingly of the fancy ladies. She was identifying with the slaves. So was I. It was not a matter of race but of class, although we never explicitly used either term. We identified with the slaves who toiled like draught animals and not with the plantation aristocrats who were so lavishly served. We were poor. There would never be anyone fanning us during hot weather.

Mamma spent all day at the dress factory, drilling buttonholes onto stacks of children's clothes. I once promised her that someday I would earn lots of money so that she could live in leisure, a vow that heartened her more because of its expression of concern than because she believed she would live to see the day. Much to my grief, soon after I turned seventeen she died, still employed in the same shop—a victim of that faulty heart that had given her such trouble during my birth. She was only forty-three.

She died in a large overcrowded understaffed ward of a run-down public hospital at a time when my father and I had great difficulty meeting her medical bills. No one had told me how sick she was. I felt a bitter pain in my heart when I saw her wasted away on a rickety narrow bed in that dingy congested ward, her sunken, once-beautiful blue eyes filled with sadness. Suddenly I realized I was going to lose her.

In the years before her death she had shown such concern about keeping up the monthly payments on her life insurance policy. Were she late a day or two, she would make a special trip to the company office to deliver the payment. Why such diligence? At the time of my birth, the doctors had told my father that because of her heart condition, mother had only about fifteen years left to live. (She lasted seventeen years.) Toward the end of her life, as she was getting seriously ill, she said to me, "I know I'm living on borrowed time." Having no knowledge of the doctor's prognosis, I emphatically objected: "Don't talk like that, Mom."

She faithfully continued payments on her life insurance because it was going to be something, the one thing, she could leave to her family. When she died, sure enough, her policy was in perfect order. An insurance agent came to the house and gave us an impenetrable rundown of the policy's arcane stipulations. Then he gave my grieving father a check for the meager sum of $200: Mamma's gift to us after the insurance connivers got their cut.

೮೦

15/ All Sorts of People

In 1940 we lived on 119th Street, west of Third Avenue, in a cold-water flat. At that time the household saint of our Italian home was a Jew named Sammy Silverman. A pudgy man in his fifties, owner of a jewelry store on Third Avenue, Sammy was a prosperous but lonely bachelor who lived with his nagging sister and brother-in-law in a ritzy downtown apartment. I once spent an overnight there and it seemed quite classy to my untutored eye.

To get away from his sister and her husband, Sammy would have dinner at our house every Sunday—with my father usually serving as cook. Sammy appreciated my father's culinary talents, as did we all. After eating, Sammy would take a quick nap in the rocking chair ("forty winks" was the old standby expression he used). Then he would engage in several hours of pinochle or poker with Poppa and Mike Cohen, a haberdasher and another Jewish bachelor. Other card players included Rocky, a tough-looking, but essentially benign Italo-American (whose last name I never knew); and Phil Santori, an aging Italian bachelor who lived with his mother.

Another occasional participant was Jack Jordan, a charming Irish American who sang melodious Irish ballads. Jack was "keeping company" with Angie DeLuci, a close friend of my mother's. Angie eventually corralled Jack at the altar. They rode off into the sunset with Angie in the saddle, spurring Jack ever onward.

My father was an excellent pinochle player, knowing when and how to bid, and able to track what cards had been played. A less formidable player was old Phil Santori, who struggled with a severe tremor in his voice and twitches in his eyes. From serving in the U.S. Army in World War I, he suffered "shell shock," so my parents informed me in hushed tones when Phil was not present. It was also said that he had been gassed. I questioned Phil about his war experiences. In sparse and halting sentences, he would offer fleeting images of the terrors of trench warfare: living with rats and lice, the night sky lit up by flares and artillery explosions, a man's leg flying in the air—riveting stuff for an action-hungry kid.

But what about the horrible something that damaged Phil's nerves and health for the rest of his life? I knew enough not to ask him about that and never did he mention it.

Of our many friends, Sammy Silverman occupied a special place. Besides the Sunday gatherings, he occasionally would take my mother and me to the movies when my father was working an extra shift as a bartender. It was Sammy who gave me my first job at age seven. After school I would sweep the sidewalk in front of his jewelry store, a task that took about ten or fifteen minutes, in exchange for a few coins. After several weeks I decided to call it quits. As an employer Sammy was generous and good natured but the job was boring and—how shall I say it—seriously lacking in career opportunities. More to the point, it cut into my precious after-school playtime.

One day I walked into the house to find my father standing in the kitchen with a pained expression on his face and my mother sitting at the table in tears. They just got news that Sammy had died from an intestinal complication. Our family had lost a special friend.

Sammy's sister immediately accused us of killing him with "all that rich Italian food." If true, it was as good a way to go as any. (The charge stung my mother.) I suspect sister-girl's constant nagging played a part in sending Sammy to his grave, as did her own table offerings of deep-fried potato latkes, and all that cooking with *schmaltz* (chicken fat) instead of olive oil.

Another friend of ours was Jack Bischoff, a big, good-natured taxi driver also a plumber at times. When I was fourteen or so, I went out on a weeklong job as his assistant, repairing busted water pipes at an upstate vacation resort.

Contrary to the prevailing stereotype, Jack was a Jew who couldn't handle money. He was easily preyed upon by various vipers, including his ex-wife (herself a Sicilian). Taking advantage of his easygoing nature, they would filch from him and never pay him back. Luckily my father was someone Jack could trust. Poppa started depositing Jack's earnings in a savings account for him, making him less likely to be targeted by hustlers. At the end of the year, instead of being broke, Jack had a comfortable stash in the bank. Eventually he and my father pooled their respective savings in order to get their own taxi medallion (in the days before medallions were astronomically priced), enabling them to drive an independent cab for some years.

I never heard my parents utter anti-Semitic or racist remarks. My mother's view was: "There's good and bad in all groups." And I even once heard my father tell a Southern acquaintance that forcing "the coloreds" to the back of the bus or into separate waiting rooms was no way to run a society. In 1955 when I told my father that I was considering marrying a Jewish girl, he said that was fine with him. I could even marry a "colored girl" if I wanted to, he added as an afterthought. Still, in later years he grew resentful toward "the coloreds" and "the Spanish," meaning respectively African Americans and Puerto Ricans, for supposedly living free off welfare and causing more than their share of crime (see chapter 40).

On the individual level Poppa seemed oblivious to race. Even in his later years he was friends with a fellow taxi driver, Henry, an articulate intelligent African American whom I met only briefly and liked instantly. My father proudly said of him, "A terrific fella. He put two kids through college driving his cab."

It has often been said that many people are against prejudice in the abstract but when face-to-face occasions arise, their bigotry shows through. Often, however, I also have seen the converse: people who nurse a generalized grievance against minority groups who then get along just fine on a face-to-face level with individuals from those same groups.

My father's brother, Nick, an auto mechanic, offered a striking example. He would badmouth every group on the planet. Then one day in 1953 or so, while he and a few other relatives were sitting in front of their house in the Bronx, an elderly African-American man approached. The man chose to give a wide berth, stepping into the gutter as he passed by. Uncle Nick was aghast. "What are you doing?" He leaped up, took the old man's arm, and ushered him back onto the sidewalk, explaining to him most insistently that he had every right to pass "just like anybody else." Everyone sitting around the stoop seemed to agree with my uncle.

I thought well of him for doing that. It made me think that maybe there was some hope for humanity — or at least for my family.

Another racial incident from earlier years sticks in my memory. Two African-American teenagers, looking quite unoffending, were walking westward on my block, from First Avenue toward Second Avenue. Their goal most likely was to get beyond Lexington Avenue into the safer (for them) passages of Black Harlem. Suddenly four or five of our street toughs surrounded them. Another came running into the group and slammed into the two youths, shouting with menacing glee. The two boys looked terrified. They were about to get seriously roughed up.

I was only about eleven years old and unable to intercede but I started wishing someone would. And someone did. From out her basement apartment came a poorly dressed, robust, high-spirited, immigrant Italian woman, whose name I did not know but whom I had seen many times. Hers was one of the very poorest families on the block. Her kids were often seen sitting on the sidewalk barefoot and dirty faced.

"You leave-ah dose boys alone!" she shouted in her Italian accent. "They more better than you! You hit them, I'm-ah gonna hit you!" The bullies were not prepared to deal with a furious middle-aged neighborhood woman. They released the two "intruders." No onlookers showed disapproval toward her. But, as I recall, none openly joined with her against the street bullies. Given their chance, the Black youths cut a swift departure.

~ *Part 3: The School* ~

16/ "Eyes Glued to the Head in Front of You"

The grade school we attended, like other institutions of captivity, invested much energy in maintaining dominion over the child, with little time or talent left for educational endeavors. Authority was omnipresent, a stream of warnings and petty scolds.

In first grade there was no afternoon activity of any kind. The afternoon session began when we returned from lunch at 12:30 PM and continued until 2 PM (First graders went home at 2 PM instead of the usual 3 PM) For that entire one-and-a-half-hour afternoon period we were forced to sit upright and motionless on hard wooden seats, with hands folded on our desks and "eyes glued to the head in front of you." We could neither speak nor read nor color in our coloring books, nor move our heads or limbs in any way, a kind of torture delivered upon the defenseless.

Meanwhile, the teacher would sit and read a magazine or do her nails, getting paid-in-full for an afternoon of invisible pedagogy. She would glance up occasionally only to chide some child for squirming on the hard wooden seat. I remember the feeling of dread that accompanied those joyless endless afternoons. None of us had an easy time of it but the liveliest children suffered the most for they were least able to successfully muffle themselves.

It was a public school obsession that penmanship be pursued with perfect uniformity by every child. There was a fixed dreary writing style known as the "Palmer Method," involving all sorts of requisite flourishes, none of them particularly attractive; each letter and its offshoots had a designated height, and all letters had to have the same tilt, all designed for right-handed application. We left-handed children were required to learn to write with our right hands.

~ Learning Moronics ~

Before starting school, I was given a small blackboard by my mother. It had a paper scroll atop it containing the alphabet. I began to copy the alphabet letters on the blackboard and teach myself the sounds of each letter, guided by whatever passing adult I could flag down to tell me how specific letters and words were pronounced. Within a short time I could recite the alphabet and sound out some words.

When I began in the first grade I was given a Dick and Jane reader that contained sentences like: "Look, look, see Spot run." "Bow wow! said Spot." "Run, run, Spot, said Dick." We pupils were repeatedly made to read aloud and in unison from these same few books. One day I told my mother to open one of the readers. And while she read along silently page after page, I recited the entire book to her from memory. Rather than being impressed, she was puzzled, feeling something more needed to be done with me but she didn't know what.

Control and conformity remained the order of the day. Running was a sin. To be found in the hallway without a pass was a felony. The most innocent forms of horseplay were treated as capital offenses. Any pupil who raised a sensible but critical question about some procedure was suspected of being an insurrectionist.

One begged for the privilege of leaving the room in order to go to the toilet. If the request were made too often (once or twice) one was told to "get a note from your doctor," a piece of advice none of us quite understood. To sum up: As preschoolers we could not read or write. Then when we went to school we discovered we also could not run, walk, or talk—not to mention even more basic bodily functions.

Being treated like imprisoned little animals, we often acted as such, indulging in various unruly outbursts, thereby justifying the need for further restrictive measures. In this way does repression create the conditions for its own justification. The authority imposed upon us showed a disregard not only for our energetic bodies but for our personal sensibilities. Defiance often became our only means of maintaining self respect.

In grade school we working-class, Italian-American children were exposed to glimpses of the Other World. Our tattered storybooks offered pictures of well tailored, blond youngsters with executive-looking fathers and slim, American-beauty mothers, children who chased butterflies through green meadows and said things like "Good morning, Mr. Robin Red Breast" to birds in the trees.

The only experience we East Harlem kids had talking to birds was cursing at the flocks of pigeons that occasionally circled above the tenement rooftops to victimize us with their oddly well-timed collective incontinence.

∞

17/ *The Teacher Creature*
Our grade school teachers were so thoroughly marinated in their own middle-class prejudices that they could not muster much regard or understanding for the ways of working-class kids. Our presence made them almost as miserable as their presence made us. Like us, they were serving time.

Looking back now, I feel a certain sympathy for some of my teachers. These were women who had known the genteel cultivation of college and travel. They dwelt in a realm beyond East Harlem, yet had to journey to a dreary public school to spend their days with slum kids who were not the answers to their dreams.

One of our teachers, Miss Rosenthal, a wispy middle-aged woman with thick glasses, occasionally tried to imbue us with a pride in our ethnic heritage. To her credit, she talked about the glories of Italian art and music, the mysteries of Mona Lisa's smile and how the blood drained from Michelangelo's arm as he lay on the scaffold painting the pope's ceiling. Her Italy was a vast museum, a summer outing, and a charming operetta. It bore no resemblance to the ragged, impoverished *meridionale* from which our families had fled. Nor was it East Harlem, the only Italy we children knew. If Miss Rosenthal had said less about Donatello and more about DiMaggio, she would have done better at stirring our ethnic pride.

For all her good intentions Miss Rosenthal committed serious errors. She made big Gino Santini stay in school an extra hour two days straight for punishment and penmanship drill even when, in anguish, he told her he would lose his job at the grocery store if he wasn't there by 3:15 PM. Shocked that one so young should be working, and convinced that learning how to write would benefit Gino far more than putting in time at a store, she would not yield to his entreaties. It was also she who scolded impoverished Joey Napoli for wearing a rag of a sweater in the winter: "Tell your parents to get you a coat." Joey's only answer was, "I'm not cold."

Then there was the eponymous Miss Munster, who sat and glared at us with menacing eye. Every day as it approached noon and hunger began to gnaw within us, she would remove a richly layered sandwich from her bag and proceed to devour it. We children had to sit and watch as every savory morsel disappeared into her voracious mouth. Miss Munster also had the habit of taking this or that troublesome boy out into the hall and banging his head against the wall, then slapping him hard across the face several times. She had her favorite victims. I luckily was selected only once for such shock treatment.

The one truly noxious teacher in grade school was Grace A. Meyer, a high-strung nail-biting stocky woman in her late forties or early fifties, whose thick freckled hands swung out at us without warning, sending heads ringing and eyes tearing. These assaults were supplemented with verbal attacks. She called us "riffraff" and repeatedly informed us that we lived "in houses not homes." She talked proudly of her German Protestant antecedents and her "dear father" who had been a lawyer in Ohio. She made known in various ways that her ethno-class background was better than ours.

Miss Meyer repeatedly instructed us to "tell your parents to speak English at home." English is exactly what most of our parents, including mine, already spoke at home, especially to their children. I don't recall her ever teaching us any English grammar or vocabulary in class. Instead of worrying about our speaking English at home, she could have taught some English at school.

Instead, Miss Meyer spent most of our classroom time rambling on incoherently, flitting from one subject to another in a stream of consciousness that I often found pointless. Occasionally, if one or another student got on her nerves, she would toss him into the classroom closet where he would have to sit in the darkness for an extended amount of time.

She once asked a group of us a question. I proceeded to blurt out an answer but was interrupted when she whacked me in the face, knocking my glasses off and breaking them. The next day my mother came to class and asked for an explanation and payment for the glasses. Miss Meyer tried to lie her way out of it, insisting that I had acted unruly. Still, she gave my mother the money for a new pair of glasses. I remember Mamma saying to her, "Something's wrong here. My child doesn't want to come to school in the morning. He was never that way before." Miss Meyer was quick to inform mother that I was seriously disturbed. This was one of her favorite themes: I was an "ill child," even though my parents, classmates, and other teachers did not seem to think so.

I am so grateful that Ritalin and all the other abusive and damaging psycho-medications produced by a profit-driven pharmaceutical industry had not yet been developed. Today with their aggressive marketing, the pharmaceutical firms—assisted by dangerously irresponsible psychiatrists—continually expand the criteria for mental illness so that one of every sixty-six Americans, many of them perfectly normal people, now take psycho-meds. For children over the last two decades there has been a startling thirty-five-fold increase. As of 2011 "mental illness" was purportedly the leading cause of disability in children.[6]

No doubt Miss Meyer would have eagerly handed me over to the tender mercies of the drug pushers in white coats.

~ How Miss Meyer Remained Pure ~
In those days almost all grade school teachers were women and most were unmarried. Matrimony usually led to retirement from teaching. Once married, the teacher was expected (but not required) to leave her profession in order to devote herself fulltime to domestic bliss and wifely duties. A pupil once asked Miss Meyer if she was married. "Of course not," she snapped. "I'm not Jewish. Only Jewish teachers get married." When I reported this strange comment to my mother, she answered angrily "Too damn bad about her! Who does she think she is! " I liked Mamma's critical response—mostly because I so disliked Miss Meyer.

What I resented about school, besides the abuse and confinement, was the insufferable boredom. On those rare occasions when I chanced upon something that interested me, I was usually

---

[6] Robert Johnson, "Business Insider," 20 July 2011; http://www.rawstory.com/rs/2011/07/20/.

not allowed to pursue it. I once was punished by Miss Meyer for reading a children's book about American presidents when I should have been performing one of the many idiot time-killing projects set before us. One thing about school I always disliked: we were rarely allowed to read. (Study hall was not offered until high school.) In order to engage my intellectual interest I had to escape from the institution that was supposedly devoted to intellectual endeavor.

It was my misfortune to have Miss Meyer as my teacher for three terms in a row (1.5 years). My lively and playful demeanor was more than she could tolerate, and I became one of her favorite targets. It reached a point where I would feign illness to avoid going to school (and be able to stay home and read *Adventure Magazine* and other pulp fiction).

Miss Meyer's certainty that I was not a well child became a self-fulfilling prophecy. By the third term under her sway (sixth grade), I developed a nervous twitch which the doctor diagnosed as "St. Vitus Dance" but which was actually a case of "Miss Meyer Madness," a condition that disappeared immediately after I departed from her class and entered junior high school.

℥

18/ School for Patriots

Teachers like Miss Meyer taught us to dislike our ethnic identities, our class origins, and our very existence as spirited children. Our Italian working-class antecedents—as revealed in our speech, deportment, and physical appearance—earned a subtle but certain disapproval. We were advised to avoid gusto in our voices and animation in our movements, stand straight and sit stiffly, to be, so to speak, proper Anglo-American prototypes.

Also in grade school we were taught the religion of Americanism, complete with its hymns (Star-Spangled Banner); its sacred symbols ("the stars and stripes"); its rituals and incantations

(Pledge of Allegiance, patriotic cheers and slogans); its harbingers and prophets (Paul Revere, Patrick Henry); its martyrs (Nathan Hale, Abraham Lincoln); its early Church Fathers (Washington, Jefferson, Madison); its Judases and apostates (Benedict Arnold, John Wilkes Booth); and its myths of divine origin (Bunker Hill, Boston Tea Party).

I and my classmates were treated to a variety of tales about America's territorial expansion, stories of an inspirational quality that suffered from few of the troublesome encumbrances proffered by historical reality. The view I had of "Indians" (Native Americans) I owed to Hollywood. They were savage "redskins" who massacred peaceful decent White settlers. And nothing I learned at school contradicted that image. America was a land that was "tamed" and "settled" by civilized White pioneers.

Likewise my view of slavery owed far too much to the perspective of the plantation owner. Abolitionists were represented as meddlesome troublemakers. Miss Meyer allowed that slaves were occasionally treated "unfairly," as when children were sold off from their parents. But in general, she emphasized, slaves were well taken care of, a view that was pretty much the general opinion. To us youngsters, the African American was either that laughable Sambo shuffling and tap dancing across the silver screen or mumbling "Yawssuh" on the radio, or that "menace" who occupied the interior wilderness west of Lexington Avenue.

World War II was blazing away in full force. Miss Myer's biggest fear was that the Axis powers might win and *Japanese* soldiers would run amok through America's communities. "Do you want to see your mothers and sisters carried off and *married* to Japanese soldiers?" (She could not, of course, get herself to say "*raped* by Japanese soldiers.") Like a backwoods crowd of rednecks being harangued by the local Klan leader, we would shake our heads and murmur in throaty tones, "No, Miss Meyer. No. No."

During P.S. 85's general assembly, our principal and other teachers urged us to join in the effort to beat the Axis by collecting scrap metal and old newspapers "from all the garbage in the neighborhood," to be recycled for the war industry, which we did. And each week in school assembly we became regular little soldiers, singing "Remember Pearl Harbor," "The Halls of Monte-zuma," "Anchors Away," "Those Caissons Go Rolling Along" and other military musical masterpieces.

Miss Meyer could never free herself from the suspicion that a classroom inhabited by Pagano and Pellegrini, DeLuca and D'Amico, lacked a genetic star-spangled fervor, especially in a war that found Italy on the wrong side.

This was farthest from the truth. Our heroes were not Hitler and Mussolini but Robert Taylor, John Wayne, and a host of other Hollywood stars, the heroic American warriors of the silver screen. When the fighting leatherneck bayoneted a Japanese soldier with words like "Take that you slanty-eyed yellow monkey! It's from the folks back in Iowa!" our Saturday matinee movie audience of Mediterranean scions shrieked as happily and wildly as any kids in Des Moines. And we experienced the death of every American soldier as a personal loss, complete with plaintive background music.

It was reassuring to see cowboy heroes like John Wayne take time off from slaughtering "redskins" in order to channel their murderous energies into exterminating those "sneaky little yellow nips" on Bataan and Iwo Jima. The Japanese were much like the Indians: unspeakably cruel and bloodthirsty. Yellow skin was as bad--if not worse--than red skin.

The Germans, it seemed to me, were portrayed as somewhat less cruel and more human. True they were capable of showing unmistakable signs of enmity such as goose stepping, speaking in snarling accents, barking orders, and shooting anyone who annoyed them. But it did not escape us that they were represented as being of the same species as the rest of us, indeed, of the same race. (None of us had yet heard of Auschwitz.)

~George Washington, Italian Style~

For at least two generations, Italian Americans felt the tension of being marginalized ethnics whose families arrived in the USA "on a banana boat" rather than on the Mayflower. We were taught to honor "our Founding Fathers," Washington, Adams, Jefferson, et al., who were not at all our "fathers," icons of a dominant culture that was slathered upon us. This might explain why many Italo-Americans found such amusement in this joke:

Q. What did George Washington say when he was crossing the Delaware?

A. *"Sono cazz' e fredd' "* [My cock is freezing].

Then came the follow-up:

Q. And what did the Indian say who was coming the other way in a canoe?

A. *"Ah, pure tu sei italiano!"* [Ah, so you too are Italian.]

That the great American hero, George Washington, making his fearless way across ice-ridden waters, would complain—in Italian—about his private parts freezing was the cause of much iconoclastic merriment. That an Italian Indian should link up with him only added to the absurdity and mirth. (Maybe you have to be Italian American to find it so amusing.)

The war offered us Italian kids a chance to feel like fully red-blooded Americans, no longer burdened by a sense of inferior marginal status. We embraced a furious brand of patriotism, *plus royale que le roi.* Who would dare challenge our Americanism when we fervently waved the stars and stripes in their faces and showed ourselves to be more American than the Americans. Our yahoo super patriotism easily equaled the kind found among old stock White Protestant children, including Mayflower descendants, but it was more vociferous, filled with that particular kind of insistence that is symptomatic of insecurity and overcompensation.

With the atomic destruction of Hiroshima and Nagasaki, we had evidence that the forces of the righteous had prevailed. America had emerged victorious. God finally showed enough good sense to be on our side. It was my unexamined faith that the United States acted only with benevolent intent and beneficial effect, the shining light and hope of all mankind. This was the faith of a grade school child in 1945 and remains today the faith held by many beguiled Americans.

৪১

19/ Producing Proper Citizens

We learned other values in grade school and junior high to supplement the lessons in jingoism and authoritarianism. We learned that it was considered better to work in a big office than as a laborer, better to live in the starched antiseptic suburban world of Dick and Jane than in fecund East Harlem.

We were urged to study hard in order to "get ahead" and "better yourself." This betterment was almost always defined in terms of material advancement, winning out against others on the job market, and rarely as a dedication to the less fortunate, to social causes and mutual betterment through cooperative efforts. Never was it suggested that "bettering yourself" might entail some essential changes in the privileged systems of power and wealth that limited our lives in ways we never fully grasped.

The few attempts at practicing "democracy" came when a teacher would say something like "let's have a vote on whether Vincent or Anthony will be blackboard monitor this week." Rather than eagerly exercising our sovereignty, many of us would refrain from raising our hands when the tally was taken, a situation that displeased the teacher. Since voting is equated with democracy and democracy is a supreme blessing, then there had to be something wrong with those who lacked enthusiasm for elections and not with the content of the elections themselves.

Actually, as I think back, insofar as they taught us a certain skepticism about the power of the ballot box and a certain hesitation about giving ourselves to meaningless participation when the issues are anemic and the choices are empty, the electoral charade we played in the classroom was the most realistic part of our political education.

At one point during my grade school education, both my parents devoted themselves full time to running a neighborhood grocery store, a business venture that failed after a year or so. Needing someone to take care of me, they sent me to live with my mother's sister, my Aunt Lucy, in the Bronx where I attended a school that might be described as middle-class. The students (mostly Jewish along with a scatter of Irish, Anglo-Protestants, and other groups) were rarely rowdy. The student body consisted of both boys and girls unlike East Harlem where schools were segregated by gender. In the Bronx school, teachers never hit their pupils. Classrooms, desks, and books were in better repair. Everything had the appearance of being nicer.

Yet, the control over our lives, while more humanely administered than at P.S. 85, was almost as persistent. The brittle threat of poor grades replaced the threat of Miss Meyer's solitary confinement closet. At the Bronx school the boys and girls were spurred on by gold stars, merits, demerits, and other such candy-ass judgments that would not impact heavily upon the street boys of East Harlem. Coming from homes where "success" meant something, the Bronx pupils were goaded on by the fear of failure. We slum kids were not worried about losing the race, since it seemed we never really left the starting line.

Tattling to teacher about a fellow pupil's misconduct was a standard practice among the "better socialized" children in the Bronx. Such tattling was an unheard of betrayal in East Harlem and was likely to invite an after-school fistfight. No doubt the slum children of East Harlem suffered a more taxing abuse than middle-class children in the West Bronx. Still I felt no particular envy for the latter.

When I returned home after a year at Aunt Lucy's, I neither missed the Bronx nor welcomed East Harlem. But I was happy to be living with my parents again.

~ *Part 4: Coming of Age Stuff* ~

20/ *The Natural Superiority of Girls*

In East Harlem we preadolescent street boys treated girls poorly—as measured by today's standards. Like crazed creatures we would whoop wildly into their rope jumping games, grabbing the rope and running off with it as if it were a war trophy. The girls' furious shrieks of protest only added to our delight. Girls also made marvelous snowball targets. Again their protests and their attempts at scurrying for cover only added to our glee.

Girls definitely were creatures from another planet. Even then it struck me how different their conversations were from ours. The girls gossiped with each other about each other and about everyday happenings, talking in a mature manner of intimacy and intricacy that reminded me of grown-up talk.

In contrast, we boys concentrated upon more worldly and scientific subjects such as: Can a tiger kill a lion? Can an elephant stop a tank? Can a hand grenade blow your entire head off? In a fistfight, is it better to aim for your opponent's nose, mouth, or eyes? and other such edifying topics. One older guy advised several of us youngsters that should we ever find ourselves in a fight with a "nigguh," always hit him in the stomach since "nigguhs have weak stomachs because they eat lots of lousy pickled stuff." Thus spoke one of our more brilliant experts on ethnic combat.

Looking at it now, I have to conclude that females are more highly evolved members of the species than males, not only back in my grade-school days in East Harlem but today throughout the world. Males have been the predominate purveyors of war, violence, conquest, rape and sexual abuse, economic rapacity, exploitation, crime, corruption, and political-cultural-religious oppression. (I eventually wrote a book that dealt with some of these subjects.[7])

As I stumbled into my adolescence, my encounters with neighborhood girls improved, bearing far less resemblance to guerrilla warfare. Gone were the raids on rope-jumping and all the other silly teasing and bullying. Relations became more cordial, more in keeping with the times: necking on park benches, necking in hallways, pressing against a young female companion as we stood glued to each other in a vestibule or under a stairwell or wherever we could invent a semi-private space.

We learned to distinguish between "good" and "bad" girls. The good ones were the ones who did not "go all the way." The bad ones did. We all expected to marry virgins, maybe because we ourselves were virgins. (This was the 1940s.)

Our working-class Italian parents and grandparents taught us that we would have to wait until we got married to have sex. Actually, they never said a word about sex. It was just understood that we would have to wait. They instructed us to stay away from girls. It was not sex they feared but what it led to: pregnancy, illegitimate children, shotgun weddings, and other such difficulties and humiliations delivered upon the family.

ℂ

21/ A Japanese War Atrocity

One day, in junior high school, as we sat around waiting for class to begin, a classmate, Joey Paladino, held us spellbound with a "true" war story that went something like this:

---

[7] Michael Parenti, *The Culture Struggle* (Seven Stories Press, 2006) 47-87.

"There was this American soldier the Japs captured and you know how they tortured him? They took off all his clothes and tied him to a tree. Then this beautiful Japanese geisha girl, a real piece of ass, started dancing in front of him, half-naked, with flimsy veils. She was a real cockteaser, specially trained to torture guys, and she teased him and danced real close and rubbed herself right on him while he was getting more and more excited. And he was going crazy and screaming, and he got so hot he begged her to stop."

"But she just kept dancing up to him and rubbing him and teasing him until he came all over himself but then *she kept doing it again and again* and he kept screaming for mercy and *he kept coming and coming* and he got weaker and weaker and he kept begging her to stop because he was going to die from all the loads he was dropping and because she made him so hot he was losing his mind. But she just laughed and the Jap soldiers laughed and she kept doing it until finally he fainted and *died!*"

Wow! It took us a moment to recover from this breathtaking report of yet another Japanese atrocity. Then came a murmur of skepticism: "Is that a true story or did you make it up?" Joey swore it was true. A cousin of his had *read it in a magazine.* That was all the documentation we needed. We were as ignorant as Joey regarding the limits of adult male sexual physiology.

Those Japanese are inhuman, we all agreed. Then we began to wonder if the war would last long enough for us to be drafted into the army and possibly meet the same terrible fate as that unfortunate American soldier. It was a frightful thought, but we were ready to risk everything for our country.

൸

22/ Loving Miss Lynch

Any memoirist who dares to write about his junior high school days must mention the "colorful" classroom characters, no matter how idiotic they were. So will I. There was Joey Riniti who lifted weights and spent the better part of his waking hours with his shirt sleeves rolled up as high as possible so that he might carry on endless narcissistic sessions caressing his own well-developed biceps.

There was Anthony Cardacci who repeatedly imitated the Hunchback of Notre Dame by tucking his lunch bag under his jacket collar, thereby creating a lump in his upper back. Then he would stick his tongue out the side of his mouth, letting some drool appear on his lips, while closing one eye and squinting out the other in a determinedly demented expression. He would begin to cry out in his best graveled Charles Laughton voice, "I am Quasimodo! Ring the bells! Ring the bells!" This role always brought us to mirth; it seemed to fit him so well.

There was Vinny D'Amico who liked to pick up dried pieces of dog shit from the street and throw them at people, including older boys. Needless to say, Vinny's targets did not take kindly to his curious disportment. Some adults and older boys would charge after him with murder in their hearts. He would run for his life laughing with terror and glee, shouting back at his pursuers some witty taunt like: "You eat shit!" He must have been caught and pummeled on occasion or at least had some close calls. The one time I saw him perform this feat he escaped with steps to spare.

Years later when I saw clips of the crazy young men in Pamplona, Spain, who risked their lives running with the bulls, I suddenly understood my deranged classmate. Vinny had found a way of injecting dangerous excitement into his humdrum life. Be that as it may, those of us who knew about his quaint habit never took to shaking hands with him.

Then there was Tony Bonatelli, a good-looking tall youth whom we called "Bone," a play on his name which he earned because he seemed to suffer from chronic tumescence. While our families preached—or assumed—abstinence as the rule, the Hollywood-dominated popular culture dangled images of leggy, busty sexpots before our hot little heads, stoking our raging hormones. But Bone got erections even in Miss Lynch's social studies class.

There was a certain mystery about this, for Miss Lynch was a seriously scrofulous, saggy, gnarled, wart-faced, ancient personage. She had a chronic cigarette cough and a hoarse croaking voice. But apparently for Bone she had what it takes.

One day while conducting the lesson, she began to stroll casually toward the back of the room, over to the side where Bone was sitting nursing his unruly member under his desk. She caught him in his criminal act with smoking gun in hand, as it were. Before he could stuff it back into his pants, she rushed up to him and delivered a ringing slap across his face. That was the appreciation she showed for the special homage he had been paying her.

"You filthy pig!" she shouted angrily.

"I couldn't help it, Miss Lynch," he whined pitifully. "It was hurting me and I was just rubbing it." A lame alibi if ever there was one, but given the circumstances could anyone have thought of something better?

"Well, don't rub it and it won't hurt," she snarled, reversing cause and effect. Bonatelli was *pleasuring* himself, something he should do neither in class nor anywhere else, as far as she was concerned.

We used to tease each other about every mishap, but no one said anything to Bone about that incident. Nor did any of us talk about it among ourselves. The mortification was just too enormous to be addressed with taunts. It also was too personal not to be shared a little by us all, if only out of sympathy for him.

∞

23/ *The Undertaker's Wife*

My one neighborhood sexual love encounter came when I was about 14 years old. It was with the undertaker's wife. It was intense and would have been perfect—except for the distance between us.

From the window of my room, while doing my homework, I could sit at my desk and gaze down across the street to a low roof that abutted the residential portion of Malgioglio's Funeral Home. Malgioglio's wife would exit the door that led directly onto the roof in order to hang the family wash on a clothesline. She was an attractive woman, full flanked, robust coloring, and sporting the loveliest legs in all of Manhattan.

Whenever she appeared, I would put my school assignments aside and fix my eyes upon her magnetic presence while nursing my throbbing desire. I did not realize that she was aware of my face (which along with my shoulders was all she could see of me) peering intently from across the way. And she probably could deduce that I was engaging in a devotional act in tribute to her.

As time went on, she seemed to be coming out to hang the wash more frequently. And I was spending more and more time in my room at my desk, impressing my parents with how studious I had become.

Mrs. Malgiolgio's movements grew increasingly elaborate. She would bend more deeply over the wash basket to pick out clothes, keeping her legs straight and her gloriously rounded posterior hoisted high. The dresses she wore seemed flimsier than ever and more responsive to the autumn breeze, swirling to teasing heights—which she made no effort to restrain. Sometimes she would "accidentally" brush her dress upward as she handled the wash, further revealing her merciless legs. Other times she came out on the roof with no wash and just seemed to putter about with some flower pots or whatever.

She would flash radiant glances in my direction, even making momentary eye contact with me. Only later did I decide that she was enjoying her exhibitionism almost as much as I was. Every afternoon I sat there hoping she would appear. I thanked God for blessing me with such wonderful neighbors as the Malgioglio family. It soon became clear to me what was going to happen next:

I meet her in the grocery store. An electrifying surge passes between us. She says to me, "Hello, aren't you the young man who lives across the street from me?" I nod calmly, the picture of self-possessed masculinity. We talk about different things. She asks me to help her with her groceries, remarking on how strong my arms look. She guesses at my age, taking me for several years older than I am. I carry the groceries into her home.

And Mr. Malgioglio? He's off at a morticians conference in Philadelphia. The children are visiting their grandmother. "It's so lonely, Mikey, my sweet one." Suddenly we are locked in a torrid embrace. We fall onto her bed in a swirl of satin sheets and silky undies. After an hour of explosive desire, we are spent. We lie there, and she sighs, uttering tender words of love to me. "You are the best I've ever had, Mikey, my darling," she coos contentedly.

Nothing like that ever happened, of course. If it had been a movie, then certainly that would have been the inevitable script. All those filmmakers, American and European, who did supposedly autobiographical coming-of-age films, would reconstruct their fantasy of the adolescent boy-hero being initiated into manhood by a beautiful older woman, a de rigueur denouement in the film world, a rarity in real life. In the United States, adult females go to jail for extending such pleasures to grateful horny fourteen-year-olds.

Returning to real life: in a matter of days, Mrs. Malgioglio canceled her roof performances. The weather was getting colder, and in any case she probably was getting bored with the peek-a-boo game. Perhaps old man Malgioglio caught wise that she was pursuing a long-distance exhibitionism and he reined her in. Or could it be that he finally bought her a clothes dryer?

In any case, as everyone knows, long distance relationships are difficult to sustain.

~ *Part 5: The Street* ~

24/ *Inventing Space*

Like most congested low-income urban areas, East Harlem was a lively but somewhat rough place to inhabit. We youngsters were "street kids" in the true sense of that term. We spent our after-school hours on the streets. Our sports consisted of box ball, punch ball, stickball, stoopball, handball, roller skating, ringalevio, Johnny-on-the-pony, kick-the-can, hide-and-seek, and the like. All these activities took place in the streets or on the sidewalks.

One nice thing about being street kids is that we were not under constant adult supervision. We were left alone enough to devise our own disportment. Most children today have little space for spontaneous frolic. If they play baseball, it is Little League, same with soccer, hockey, or whatever: they are smothered with coaches, teachers, and parents, all shouting directives and encouragement from the sidelines. The kids look miserable. In East Harlem we invented—or inherited—our own games and our own street culture. On the rare occasions when adults watched, they usually kept their distance.

As if on cue, at one time of year or another, all the kids would appear on the street with tops, and we would be spinning tops for a week or so. At another time, we would all start playing marbles right along the dirty street curbs. Weeks later everyone was flipping and trading baseball cards Then, after some "quiet" time, we would be out on roller-skates (metal ones clamped to one's shoes), spinning the asphalt as if our lives depended on it.

Very few of us could afford our own bicycles. But there was a bike store nearby and suddenly, as if orchestrated by an invisible hand, it would be bike season and we would all be tearing around the streets on rented bikes. This might be followed by the week when kites were all the rage, we would trek across the Tri-Borough Bridge to Randall's Island and fly our newly acquired kites. Who orchestrated these recreational fads, if anyone, I never knew. It seemed to have its own communal rhythm.

Our survival depended on the ability to dodge cars and stay out of serious trouble. Our gangs were informally organized, and while capable of a variety of roughhouse activities, none of us carried guns or would ever think of doing so. We were not only drug-free, we had never even heard of narcotics.

But of course we street kids did perform acts of dash and daring that sometimes went beyond the bounds of good sense. Every so often a boy would sustain serious injury by leaping from one tenement rooftop to another without quite making it, or falling while climbing fire escapes or while catwalking high walls and fences. Other mishaps included running into the path of a vehicle, or hitching a ride on the back of a trolley or bus — and falling off.

In whatever way we could, we tried to accommodate ourselves to an unaccommodating environment. The street belonged to the omnipresent automobile (of which there were not as many as today); the sidewalks belonged to the adult pedestrians, the hallways to the janitors and tenants, the storefronts to the store owners, even the schoolyard was locked up soon after 3 PM. We kids lived in the neighborhood's interstices, constantly inventing and reinventing spaces of our own: empty lots, stoops, cellars, backyards, street corners, and the fronts of abandoned stores.

The youths I knew, ages nine to nineteen or so, spent most of their time on our home block, 118th Street. We gathered on the steps of the old abandoned church or in front of the candy store or where the sidewalk widened (because two houses were built further back from the street) or on one or another large stoop or at night under the lamppost after the dice game was over, talking, joking, arguing, boasting, and kidding each other—there was no end to the verbal exchanges. Here was certain proof that we were of Italian lineage: we never stopped talking.

Conversations were always dominated by the older youths, but we younger ones, lingering on the periphery, were occasionally allowed to inject a comment or a question if we made it quick. And the older youths would usually listen and respond even if only to dismiss our utterances. Often they would try to impress us and each other with one or another kind of discourse. There were numerous times when we younger ones would gather among ourselves to talk, though our exchanges tended to be more fragmented and easily derailed by some action or distraction like throwing a rock at a rat or getting up a game of stoopball.

The older youth and some of the neighborhood men occasionally indulged in a game called *morra*, a hand flashing contest that dates back thousands of years to ancient Rome and Greece (a more complicated form of "odds and evens" and "paper, scissors, rock"). Two players would flash one, two, or more fingers out from one hand (or a clenched fist to denote "zero"), and each would shout what the sum of both hands might be. Every time a player guessed correctly the sum of fingers of both players, he would score a point. If the numbers thrown did not match the numbers shouted, no point was scored, of course.

To guess ten, a player would have to throw all five fingers out and match them with the five fingers thrown by his opponent (who might be crying out "*otto*" for eight, in anticipation that his opponent would throw out only three fingers to match his five). A ten score would never be "*dieci*"; instead it would evoke the most furious of shouts: "*Morrraaaaa!*" as if you were killing your opponent. *Morra* games were often between teams and they were played with deadly earnest with money down. The greatest joy was to shoot one's hand forward and bellow at the top of one's lungs while making a point against your opponent.

I played *morra* any chance I could, which was very seldom since it was a game reserved largely for the older boys and grown men. I most loved the savagery of the calls and the gusto of the game, part snarl and part connivance. But *morra* was never that popular among the younger kids and it seemed to die out completely by the third generation.

As we got older we ventured into larger spaces. By high school age, I and my buddies Tommy Fararo, Jimmy Foglia, and Joe Fazio became regulars with the 120th Street kids around Pleasant Avenue, partly because the handball/basketball court in their neighborhood, just off the East River, was illuminated every evening with klieg lights, allowing us to play handball and hang around the park while flirting with the local girls.

₭

25/ *Fighting with Friends*

"Carlo *Geese*! Carlo *Geese*! There's another Carlo I know on 119th St and everybody calls *him* Carlo Geese too." It was my friend Frog Eyes Martino who was laughing along with me as we puzzled over why "everyone" we knew named Carlo was nicknamed Carlo Geese. To this day I have no idea.

But there was no mystery as to why Frog Eyes, a.k.a. Froggy, had to bear his quaint moniker. He had bulging amphibian eyes that made him look like he was about to leap off the pod and into the pond.

I had several fistfights with Froggy. The last two I won handily even though he was much taller. He would make the mistake of coming at me with wide-open windmill punches, so I would quickly jab straight and hard down the middle and would land some mean ones on his nose and mouth. (By 14-years-old I was fairly practiced at boxing.)

The last fight I had with Frog Eyes I drew him into it with challenges, knowing I could beat him. After a short one-sided exchange he quit and hastily walked away clutching his face and fighting back the tears. I remember that fight with shame and regret right down to this day—because I was playing the bully, a role that did not sit well with me. Usually it was my inclination to stand up to bullies when I could. But there I was forcing him into a fight I knew I would win. Nothing at all to be proud of.

Joey Martino, a.k.a. Froggy, if you're still alive and if you ever read this book. I'm really sorry. Better yet, I hope you never see this book and have completely forgotten about me and the incident.

I wish I could have directed my energies into more beneficial channels. My mother tried unsuccessfully to stamp out my street fighting with such admonitions as: "Stop getting into fights. It doesn't matter if you win or lose, when you get home your father will give you the rest, then you'll lose for sure."

Despite such warnings I developed into a fairly good boxer thanks to the efforts of one Dominic Petroni. Stocky Dominic was a powerful and skillful puncher who took pity on me. After seeing me get my brains beaten out a few times, he took me under his hefty wing and spent some afternoons teaching me to jab straight rather than swinging wild roundhouses (as poor Froggy still did); move from side to side and lean in with your whole torso when you deliver a jab; and most essential, as Dominic put it, "Keep your eyes open when you're aiming a punch, you dumb bastard."

I reached the point where I could hold my own against boys who were bigger. They usually got the better of me but I would land enough hard punches as to make them hesitant to seek another encounter. I learned that the next best thing to victory was deterrence.

> ### ~ Your Mother's . . . ~
> We would hurl insults of the worst kind at each other but mothers were off-limits. The surest way to initiate a fistfight was to say something disrespectful about your opponent's mother. Refer to a strategic part of her anatomy or her notorious bedroom generosity and your opponent would come at you with fists flying.
>
> Years later I was relieved to see my son, Christian, attending an enlightened middle school in Vermont. Here was a more cultivated and elevated way of life away from the sidewalk brawls and mean streets of East Harlem. Then one day, Christian casually mentioned to me that he and his classmates occasionally swapped elaborate insults and got into fistfights. "Sure," he told me, "just say something like, 'Yeah I was gonna screw your mama but I didn't have the two dollars she charges,' and that gets things rolling." (*Plus ça change, plus c'est la même chose.*) Long live the male animal.

One kid I did a couple of rounds with was my classmate and friend, Tom Fararo. Tommy was a bright student with whom I struck up a friendship partly because of our common interest in books. The last boxing match I had with him was a sidewalk contest with gloves. He was substantially taller. I kept trying to reach his face while he kept bopping me on the head rather effortlessly. He proved the more effective fighter with a jab that easily outreached mine. Presiding over the match was Dominic Petroni who later reluctantly but emphatically informed me that Fararo was the better fighter and I should give up trying to equal him, advice that I sensibly heeded. In any case, Tommy never went looking for fights.

Dominic, however, had thoughts of his own about sparring with Fararo. As Tommy described it many years later, Petroni invited him to his family's apartment saying, "My mother wants to see me box." They put on the gloves and performed an exhibition bout in front of an audience of one or more Petroni family members. No surprise that slender Tommy came off second best as hefty Dominic delivered him a bloody nose. Mama Petroni must have been very proud of her darling boy.

Dominic Petroni had visions of becoming a professional fighter. But beating up neighborhood kids was not quite the same as making it in the big ring. Rumors were that Petroni did enter Golden Gloves competition but ended up with just some hard knocks and a little punch drunk. In time, he reportedly sank into low-level shady dealings.

Years later, Tom Fararo, once again living in East Harlem after a stint in the Air Force, was walking down a street. A disheveled down-and-out derelict approached him and exclaimed, "Tom!" Fararo looked at him quizzically and then walked on. Who could that be? The bum turned away and walked off with a sad dejected look on his face. Only a couple of blocks later did Tommy realize with a shock that it had been none other than Dominic Petroni.

Dominic had become something of a neighborhood bum whose weak eyesight and injuries sustained in the ring did nothing to improve his life chances. He believed in the American Dream. He tried in the way he knew best, with his fists, to make the dream come true. His failure story is one of the many that never find their way into the mainstream media.

Tommy Fararo and I remained friends right into our college and post-graduate years. During high school days he introduced me to the work of Ernest Hemingway, F. Scott Fitzgerald, Thomas Wolfe, and Eugene O'Neill. The fact that he was reading them and telling me about these writings gave me the courage and interest to try reading them myself. I even ventured on my own to take on Oscar Wilde, Thackeray, Dickens, Dostoyevsky, and the book that transported me to another world: Tolstoy's *War and Peace*.

After dropping out of college and spending four years in the Air Force, Tommy came back to East Harlem with Irene, his nice

German wife. He then finished his undergraduate work, went on to get a doctorate in sociology, and in time became one of the nation's leading mathematical sociologists, producing esoteric works hailed as brilliant by the highly select numbers of academics who mastered such pursuits.

I always thought well of Tom Fararo. He was a fair-minded person of calm disposition. Some seventy years after I first met him at P.S. 85, Tom and I are still in contact with each other. He lives in retirement outside Pittsburgh, Pa., now a widower.

Not long ago we had an exchange in which I argued that he had been a most beneficial intellectual influence and oasis in my life, introducing me to various quality authors. No, he begged to differ, it was I who had the crucial influence on him, directing him to go on to graduate school and a life of scholarship. Both of us were referring to different instances, and both of us were correct.

One nice thing I remember about Tommy. After crying my eyes out all morning the day my mother died, I went to his house to tell him the sad news and much to my surprise he burst into tears, a few quick sobs. My mother had always treated him kindly and he well appreciated it.

∽

26/ Italian Names, American Games

In the East Harlem of the 1940s, the names that street kids dubbed each other could be merciless because they often referred to physical attributes that were less than flattering, as the example of Frog Eyes Martino demonstrated.

One kid, Louie Zuccatto, had a big nose, so of course he was called Louie Nose, or sometimes, just Nose. Louie was Nose to those who were older and bigger than he. We younger and smaller kids dared not address him in that manner.

In fact, with the younger kids whom he gathered around in his gang, including me, Louie Nose insisted upon being called Killer.

Here one sees the influence of Hollywood and radio dramas (there was no television just yet). Why would any sane youngster want to be called *Killer*? Well, if he happened to be a street kid in East Harlem, a name like Killer obviously had a certain cachet, borne by someone who was not to be messed with—unlike, say, someone called Bubbles or Four-Eyes or Candy Ass.

One of the older youths had an odd floppy-foot way of walking, so he was crowned Anthony Feet. ("Anthony" was usually pronounced "Ant-nee.") A buddy of his named Patty, who wore a brace on his shriveled leg and walked with a limp, was called Patty Bones, a name he seemed to wear proudly.

Then there were the heavyweights: Nicky Fat and Tiger Fat. The first of Tiger Fat's two nicknames came not from any feline quality in his physiognomy but from his family name: Tigerelli. Another nickname derived from a family name was Sonny Pisciatelli, whom the older boys called Sonny Pish or just Pish (which meant "piss"). We younger ones ran a risk if we addressed him as Pish

Both Nicky Fat and Tiger Fat were hefty, chunky, solidly built, overweight but without many blubbery folds, more like football linemen. Both were powerful stickball players, heavy hitters quite literally. Then came BoBo Pellegrini, commonly known as BoBo Fat, a redundant name if ever there was one, because to us Bo meant fat, and BoBo meant doubly so, and BoBo Fat meant really seriously off the scales, as he certainly was, hence the tri-nomina overkill.

One Halloween night when we were all dressed up in costumes, BoBo Fat appeared as a derelict in baggy old pants, a tattered jacket, and a chewed-up cap. He had covered his face with soot and ash to add to his grimy penniless aspect. His heavy hulk and shabby costume gave the appearance of a homeless derelict. (This was back in the pre-Reagan days when homeless people were relatively rare sights, even in poor neighborhoods.) Hobo

BoBo lay on his side on a widened portion of sidewalk near the corner of 118th Street and Second Avenue, making snorting, hawking, and hacking sounds like an old wino. It was a sterling performance.

The payoff for us was to stand nearby and watch the reactions of the unknowing adults who walked by, some shaking their heads and others commenting with sad sympathy, "Look at that. What a shame, poor man." This gave us kids no end of delight. We were putting one over on the adults. A small victory, out-manipulating the manipulators.

The street kids my age called me Mikey and Mike. Both Mikey and Mike are of course standard derivatives of Michael, hardly worthy of being considered original nicknames. Most of the older guys on the block called me Lefty because I was left-handed as was evident when I played ball or boxed. My mother taught me to use eating utensils with my right hand which I still do. It was considered bad manners to eat left-handed at the table. In many Italian families in the 1930s and 1940s left-handedness was treated as a kind of disability or weird trait in need of urgent correction. *Sinistro* in Italian could pertain to the left-hand or could also mean sinister or evil (more so *sinistra*). Among some of the superstitious peasants a left-handed child could also be indicative of an *illegitimate* child—which was worse than evil, it was shameful. It meant your mother had been around the block a few times. Not that my father displayed any visible worries in that regard.

The public school too had little tolerance for my southpaw proclivities. In my first days in grade school the teacher would rap my knuckles with a ruler whenever I picked up a pencil or pen in my left hand, the "wrong" hand. We wrote, saluted the flag, turned the page, and shook hands all with our right hands. Conformity was king even if it meant rewiring a student from verso to recto.

From grade school until about my sophomore year in high school I would on infrequent occasions be afflicted with a slight stammer. I read somewhere that a high percentage of stammerers and stutterers were left-handed kids who had been forced to act right-handed for various skilled practices.

Another outcome of this idiotic preoccupation of parents and teachers who worried about my *sinistra* tendencies is that I have spent the rest of my life being directionally challenged, making left turns when I should be going right, or telling someone to go right when I meant left, a confusion that has almost led to some serious traffic accidents.

ò

27/ *Bulls and Other Hustlers*

It wasn't just the kids who were blessed with sobriquets. So were the local racketeers. One of them, a short little character, was fittingly called Banjo. He was endowed with a round flat face and circular rimless glasses to match, as if one could pluck a tune on his nose. He also had a nervous bouncy manner that might suggest banjo music.

Probably the most forbidding looking racketeer was Clam, a tall bulky carnivore in an ominous overcoat. He had a grim manner, punctuated by a wide but thin-lipped mouth that sealed the bottom of his broad face from ear to ear, indeed suggesting a giant clam.

The police had their own nicknames; they were called "bulls" or "coppers" (pronounced "coppuhs"). Any bull, uniformed or plainclothes, who "pinched" (arrested) anyone over minor matters, enforcing the law in an excessive manner, with no particular benefit to anyone, was scornfully labeled a *Dick Tracy*, after the comic strip detective. There was much resentment toward the trigger-happy copper who might win promotion to detective by shooting a youth in the back as the latter fled from the scene of a minor theft.

The police were famously disinclined to confront the local racketeers but they would swoop in on ordinary neighborhood men who were shooting dice under the lamppost or doing some light nickel-and-dime card gambling on a stoop. Big, beefy, florid-faced cops of voice and appearance different from our own, representative of the power of the Outside World. Years later when James Baldwin, in one of his essays, likened the police in the Black neighborhoods of Harlem to foreign troops patrolling a hostile territory, I knew exactly what he meant. The working-class Italians of East Harlem had pretty much the same view of the police as an occupation force.

These Dick Tracys would get all bent out of shape about card games, dice games, and "playing the numbers." Most of us, however, saw gambling as nothing more than a harmless diversion—unless carried to large sums that one could not afford.

~ Police Protection (Racket) ~

The bulls ran their own protection racket against small businesspeople, bearing a smelly resemblance to the mafia's. Consider this communication I received from an old friend of mine.

"My Italian father had a shoe repair shop in the Bronx. I can't recall how often it happened, but I do recall that during the night someone, either an off-duty cop or a uniformed policeman would jiggle the doorknob to see if it was locked and leave a calling card in the door handle. Then they would come by when the store was open and expect a payment from my father. I remember more than once my father handing a couple of dollars to the cop. 'Damn Irish Micks!' I said to myself at that time (a choice of words I wouldn't use today)."

—Jack Assainte, email to me, February 2011

On 119th Street and Third Avenue I once saw a plainclothesman waiving a gun and chasing a numbers bookie down the block, shouting "Stop or I'll shoot!" Getting no cooperation, the bull pointed the gun skyward and fired. The fleeing man instantly stopped in his tracks and hurled his hands over his head. He was pounced upon, cuffed, and stuffed into a police car—a successful pinch by an intrepid Dick Tracy. The bulls were fearless in the way they pursued inconsequential minions.

As far as we knew, neighborhood hustlers like Clam and Banjo were not syndicated with the big Mafia families. There was no *capo di tutti i capi*, no boss or under-boss, no Tony Soprano or Don Corleone. In fact, the term *mafia* was unknown to us. The racketeers were never referred to as "mobsters" or "gangsters." I never saw one of them take out a gun. I doubt they carried weapons. They were not big-time killers, just small-time hustlers. Nobody in the neighborhood lived in particular fear of them. Then again, nobody went out of their way to come up against them.

The neighborhood racketeers could be seen regularly hanging around the bar on Second Avenue just around the corner from where I lived on 118th Street. Whatever "jobs" they pulled, it was usually small-time stuff, but it was enough to allow them to own cars, something relatively few families could afford in those days. The racketeers also were distinguished from the many ordinary working men in the neighborhood by the suits and fedora hats they sported as if it was always Sunday.

Despite his forbidding presence, Clam was capable of occasional levity. There was the time he was walking down the block and a grown-up was yelling at us kids for some reason. With the barest hint of a smile, Clam called out, "Leave them alone. These kids'll make good racketeers when they grow up." This was a first-rate compliment, for us kids a memorable moment that I now breathlessly pass on to the reader.

Banjo too was capable of edifying levity. One Sunday morning at about 6 AM Banjo and a friend started lighting firecrackers out on the street right across from our house. (For Banjo it was still

Saturday night.) Banjo's hardy firecracker diversion—so much a measure of the man—awakened my mother. "*Mikey!*" she exclaimed, calling my father to action. "Make him stop!"

Caught between confronting a racketeer or standing up to my angry mother, my father did not hesitate. "Hey Banjo," he called down from our window, "Whaddaya say! It's six o'clock Sunday morning!" Banjo and his companion put away their firecrackers and quietly walked off. Generally the racketeers were not looking for trouble with the community.

My father patronized the saloon just around the corner from our house. It was owned by Al Ross (Rossellini), one of the racketeers. On one occasion Poppa had some dealings with Al Ross himself. It involved his younger sister, my Aunt Anna. There was a local man who dated my young attractive aunt on one occasion. She decided that he made her uncomfortable in a creepy sort of way. So she declined any further invitations from him. This only whetted his appetite and he took to stalking her and delivering salacious overtures, causing her some trepidation.

My father brought up the matter with Al Ross. Could Al deal with the problem? Indeed. Al talked to people who knew the creep. They in turn gave the man serious warning to lay off Aunt Anna. Then Al Ross took Aunt Anna aside for a brief consultation. He assured her that she would have no further trouble. But, he added, "If you ever change your mind and start going out with him again, then you're going to be very sorry."

He was telling Aunt Anna that he would be greatly annoyed if she made his efforts look inconsequential by giving the stalker a second opportunity. Having solved the problem, he did not want his efforts undermined by her. She had nothing further to do with the man, who himself never again dared to approach her. Nothing like a word from Al Ross to concentrate the mind.

ଯ

Among the older guys who hung around 118th Street, there was Randy Bo. While not really obese, Randy was chubby enough around the face and midriff to earn the Bo. One of his eyes repeatedly went off in its own direction but no one was inclined to fashion a nickname out of that floating irregularity. For all his imperfections he had a certain intense and impressive presence. The weird eye did not stop Randy Bo from being a high scorer with the ladies. Of all the local swains, he was the most sexually active in word and deed.

Most of the older guys talked about "banging broads," telling stories about their amazing feats and devilish triumphs, going from badda bing, badda boom to *banga* bing, *banga* boom. My young unseasoned mind readily believed these tales of derring-do. Only when I got a little older did I realize that many of these amorous yarns were much improved with the telling.

Bedding women seemed to be Randy Bo's prime activity in life. We did occasionally catch a glimpse of him squiring one or another damsel along First Avenue or Second Avenue. They usually looked like they came from outside the neighborhood. In story after story we would hear how he had his way with women of different backgrounds and ethnic make-ups. Banging broads was a fulltime job that could have served Randy Bo better had it been endowed with a little more sensual joy and personal affection, not to mention occasional rest periods.

Randy did have one saving grace that registered with me. He not only was a little older than most of the other guys who loitered on our block, he also was a little more sophisticated in his observations, at least when he wasn't crowing about his conquests. He seemed to know about a lot of things that went beyond the neighborhood's narrow horizon.

One day the topic was baseball, the second most important subject for these street swains. In the middle of the chatter, I injected a comment. Having just read the *New York Daily News* sports section, I volunteered something like, "There's a new young colored pitcher named Satchemo. He's supposed to be funny with his long windup."

"Satchemo's not his real name, kid. It's Satchel, Satchel Paige, and he's not young." Randy was speaking right at me in an oddly heartfelt tone. "It's a fuckin shame he wasn't brought up to the big leagues years ago in his prime. He was kept away because of his skin color. He's in his forties now." Randy Bo went on to call Satchel Paige the greatest pitcher who ever lived. He spoke with real feeling about Satchel's exploits and the prejudice that for so long had denied this sterling athlete a chance to show his stuff in the big leagues—and denied Randy Bo the chance to see him at the height of his greatness.

Years later I read about Satchel Paige and learned that everything Randy said about him was true. Satchel was probably the greatest pitcher of all time, a legendary sports figure in his own day. Joe DiMaggio called Satchel "the best and fastest pitcher I ever faced." (DiMaggio faced Satchel's pitching during pre-season exhibition games between the Yankees and Negro teams).

During one period in 1933 in the Negro Leagues, Satchel Paige pitched 64 consecutive scoreless innings and ran up 21 straight wins—and that was against some of the finest and toughest Black hitters in Negro baseball. But because of the racial barrier he ended up being the oldest rookie to make it into the major (White) leagues, at age 42, well after his prime, and about a year after Jackie Robinson so dramatically broke the color barrier.

Randy Bo's discourse on Satchel Paige went on for a bit. I remember it with appreciation. Interestingly enough, none of the Italian boys challenged Randy's comments. One might have expected them to say something disparaging about a Black baseball star. Instead, they listened intently to Satchel Page's story without uttering a word.

~ Flash Forward ~

It is the year 2004. I am living in Berkeley, California. One day I find myself at the Berkeley Cheeseboard, a worker-owned store that makes some of the finest bread in the world and excellent pizza. True to its name, the Cheeseboard also offers an impressive array of local and imported cheeses. Since the store is a workers-collective, all its employees share in the responsibilities and decision-making. They all seem to be people of some education and political awareness.

Discounts are given to elderly people and at the end of the day, leftovers are handed out to homeless street people, of whom this great American plutocracy has produced an abundance in the last several decades.

One day Sue Anne, an attractive middle-aged blonde who worked behind the Cheesboard's pizza counter, said to me, "Michael, how about bringing around some of your Italian homeboys so I can meet one."

I started to think, not too clearly, that maybe she and Randy Bo would make a great pair. If anyone could get him to settle down and stay home at night, it would be Sue Anne. But then I realized that my Italian homeboys were all in New York and over sixty years had gone by. (Time really flies when you are trying to stay alive.) Sixty years! Randy Bo probably had long departed to that Great Bordello in the Sky.

"Sue Anne," I remarked jokingly, "by now all my Italian homeboys from the old neighborhood are either long dead or in jail."

"That's okay," she said, "I'll take the ones who are in jail." She wasn't kidding.

~ *Part 6: Priests and Politicos* ~

29/ *Jesus Was a Roman Catholic*

Like many Italians, my parents were only part-time Catholics. They did not attend Sunday mass, nor did they go to confession or take Holy Communion or believe in an afterlife. "When you're dead, you're dead. There's nothing more after this," my mother said to me (much to my shock) not long before she departed from this bruising world. My father was of the same persuasion, though perhaps a bit more upbeat: "When you die, your troubles are over."

When church-sponsored processions passed through the neighborhood, as was a common occurrence on holy feast days in East Harlem, my parents never ran out to throw coins or pin dollar bills onto the saint statues that were being shouldered by devout acolytes of the local sodality. The old Italian ladies who marched *barefoot* in the procession, while clutching rosary beads, weeping and praying loudly, were scornfully dismissed by my parents as "the fanatics."

Yet despite all this, Mom and Dad faithfully refrained from eating meat on Friday, in obedience to the then existing Catholic stricture. They both were baptized and later married in a Catholic church, and baptized their own infant son in a Catholic church. They called in a priest to perform last rites when their parents or other relatives died. They and other family members were all buried in Catholic cemeteries. Asked what their religion was, they would have said they were Catholics and believed in God.

By 1943, when I was ten years old, my parents still showed no signs of sending me off to church for catechism training. But one of my many aunts considered it urgent that I be subjected to this *rite de passage*. Most children underwent catechism when they were eight or nine. I was overdue.

My parents yielded. Questions of religious faith were secondary to questions of proper conformity. They did not want people whispering: "There go Mike and Rena. Their son is that little pagan savage who never received his First Communion and Holy Confirmation." So I was sent to catechism less to save my soul, more to save appearances.

I found Holy Rosary Church to be both inviting and a bit forbidding with its stone columns and high arched ceiling; the marble altar adorned with laces and flowers; the statues of various saints in devotional poses; the series of statuettes along the walls portraying Jesus' crucifixion (the Stations of the Cross); the smell of candle smoke, incense, and damp stone; the luminous stained-glass windows that tinted the sunlight; and the imposing statue of a large, muscular, nearly naked Christ bleeding on his cross. Presiding over it all was the Holy Virgin Mother Mary, *Madonna mia*, looking down from an immense mural over the altar, a mixture of sorrow and joy writ large upon her visage, while baby angels fluttered about her like humanoid pigeons.

I did not particularly like catechism, sitting in a cramped room with ten other boys while a priest drilled us with endless questions in return for our rote responses:

"Who made us?"

"God made us."

"Who is God?"

"God is the Supreme Being who made all things."

"Why did God make us?"

"God made us to show forth his goodness and share with us his everlasting happiness in heaven."

"Who teaches us to know, love, and serve God?"

"Jesus Christ, the son of God teaches us through the Roman Catholic church." *Through the Roman Catholic church.* No doubt about it, Jesus was a Roman Catholic. I was on the winning team.

Back and forth went the questions and answers. Catechism was much like school. We children memorized the answers to questions. The priest, like the teacher, did not have to memorize anything. He could read it all from a booklet. He sat at the head of the class, bored and slightly impatient, just like a school teacher.

More tedious than catechism were the rosary prayer sessions. Thirty captive boys and girls sat in the pews, led by Sister Mary Margaret Joseph, reciting ten Hail Marys and one Our Father then another ten Hail Marys and another Our Father, droning on and on seemingly forever. "Hail Mary, full of grace. The Lord is with thee. Blessed art thou amongst women" and so forth. They called it Holy Rosary Church for good reason.

I imagined my immortal soul to be as Sister Mary Margaret Joseph described it: a pure white glowing entity within me. I assumed it was about the size of a football, situated somewhere beneath my breastplate, close to my heart.

At birth my soul had one awful smudge on it: original sin. Everyone was born with original sin, except the Virgin Mother herself who was a product of an Immaculate Conception (so that she would not pass on any original sin to Baby Jesus). Having had the good fortune of being born a Catholic, I was able to have the unsightly original-sin smudge removed at infancy via the sacrament of baptism—as administered by a Catholic priest.

But as I advanced through life my sins accumulated: cursing, lying, disobeying my parents, entertaining salacious thoughts, eating meat on Friday, and *missing Mass on Sunday* (the most deadly sin of all, it seemed). All these wicked things delivered unsightly smudges upon my soul. Only confession could eliminate them and even then not entirely. It was like erasing dark pencil marks from a page; there always remains a trace.

If I died and my soul was too besmirched, especially with un-repentant *mortal* sins, I would go straight to hell, into a pit of fire, screaming in pain for all eternity without so much as a yearly break for an iced lemonade. The horrors of hell had a disconcert-ing effect on me when I allowed myself to dwell on such things.

But if I did enough erasing of sins by making good confessions and penance, and receiving Holy Communion and going to church every Sunday, then I would end up in *purgatory* where I could work off the sins from my impure soul by burning in the flames. But unlike hell, one's stay in purgatory would last for only a number of years of torture, after which I would be ushered up to heaven to experience *eternal* bliss. I believed every bit of this ma-niacal scenario. But then again, I was only ten years old.

On the day of my First Communion, I was dressed in a little dark suit and white tie, with a big white silk bow pinned to my arm, looking like a score of other boys as we lined up across from a score of little girls in white dresses and veils. It looked like a mass marriage of tiny people.

Kneeling at the altar I took the communion wafer into my mouth, recalling what we had been told: "During mass the priest changes the communion wafer into Christ's body, his actual living flesh. That's what you take into your mouth, children, the living flesh of our Lord himself. Leave the sacred wafer on your tongue and let it dissolve. You must never let it touch your teeth."

I pressed the wafer between my tongue and the roof of my mouth, not wanting to chew on Our Savior's living body. I gently ate my God. Jesus tasted good. Holy Communion? *Holy Cannibal-ism!*

ॐ

30/ *Paradise Lost*

Once a year a weeklong mission was conducted at Holy Rosary by the Passionist Fathers. Three evenings for the women, three evenings for the men. When I was about thirteen years old, I attended one of these three-evening missions. I found it oddly exhilarating and entertaining. The altar was ladened with bouquets and giant candles. The visiting missionaries spoke about God, sin, and the Catholic Church with a fervor seldom heard in the lackluster sermons given at Sunday mass by the parish priests.

On the last mission night, candles were passed out to all the men in the congregation. Each candle was lit and held aloft blending into the skyline of larger candles sitting high upon the altar, a majestic temple of fire amidst which knelt the black robed Passionist Father on a platform elevated close to the pulpit. Lifting high a large crucifix, he made a severe silhouette against the glitter. "Repeat after me," he exclaimed, "I denounce the devil!"

"I DENOUNCE THE DEVIL!" roared the crowd of men.

"I denounce the world!" cried the priest.

"I DENOUNCE THE WORLD!" they thundered. Why would we denounce the world? I wondered.

"I denounce the flesh!" shouted the priest. There was a moment of hesitation, then:

"I DENOUNCE THE FLESH!" To me this was another strange declaration. Yet as a production, the tableau was magnificent, a dazzling pagan splendor of blazing candles and clouds of incense, as the high priest rang the welkin and raged against demons, while the crowd chanted along, bolstered further by a sudden explosion of hard-punching organ music from the loft above and behind us. I felt as if I were in one of those South Sea movies that so transported me, starring Jon Hall and Maria Montez. I could see it all happening:

The scantily clad maiden looks lovely as she is about to be sacrificed upon the altar to the great God Ankonga. She is understandably appre-

hensive about having the pagan priest carve out her heart with a stone knife. "Jon!" she cries, her eyes fixed upon me. "Please rescue me, my darling!" I rise from my pew and push my way through the crowd, a chanting mass of people, some adorned like South Sea Islanders in brightly colored beads and flowers, others dressed like New York Italians in their Sunday best.

"Out of my way, you imbeciles!" I shout in a commanding baritone as I lift Maria Montez into my arms, feeling her loving warmth. "Quick, into my canoe." I begin to paddle away as the shouting crowd throws soda bottles at us, while the high priest stares down from the altar in a cold fury. I glide the canoe with swift faultless strokes until Maria and I reach a safe lagoon deep in the heart of Central Park.

I hold her close to me but now her face grows pensive and she pushes me away, her tiny brown hands pressing against my great hairy mat of a chest.

"No, I cannot go with you, Jon, my love. You think I am Maria Montez of Hollywood, California. But the truth is I am Princess Wannalaya of the South Seas. Your people are not my people. Our hearts are one but our ways are different. You eat spaghetti and I eat coconuts." Her eyes pool with tears.

"Oh, Maria, my folks on 118th Street will love you like their own daughter. Anyway, I like coconuts."

"No, Jon, it is right that I leave this strange island of Manhattan and return to my people and marry Momoogoo."

"Momoogoo! That skinny little clam digger! No, Maria, I mean, Princess Wannalaya. I won't let you do it."

But it is too late. The Princess disappears into the jungle as the crowd of natives gather along the shore to shout at me in their strange primitive tongue: "Stupido!" "Cretino!" "Sporco Bastardo!" "Buffone!"

In such ways did religious ceremonies ignite my young heart with transcendent scenarios.

Around that time, I became an altar boy (one of those lucky ones never molested by priests). I would serve at novenas and holy mass. In those days mass was still said in Latin (the *Missale Romanum*). So I memorized my lines in Latin usually with less than a precise understanding of what I was saying. But I still remember the life-affirming opening exchange:

Priest: *In nomine Patris, et Filii, et Spiritus Sancti. Amen. Introibo ad altare Dei.* (In the Name of the Father, the Son, and the Holy Ghost. Amen. I will go unto the altar of God.)

Altar Boy: *Ad Deum qui laetificat juventutem meam.* (To God who giveth joy to my youth.) The missal was all downhill after that.

Father Mazziato wanted me to go to Catholic school so that I might continue my religious education and eventually become a priest. The thought intrigued me. Become a priest! Be able to turn bread and wine into the body and blood of Jesus Christ. Listen to everyone's confessions and give them penance. Never worry about finding a job the way my father's entire generation worried. Best of all, priesthood was a sure ticket to heaven. How many priests went to hell, I wondered. Probably none at all.

Certainly not Monsignor Archese, the head clergyman at Holy Rosary. Archese had an aura of command about him, fortified by a white shock of hair and an aged but still handsomely rugged face. His Italian accent only enhanced his gravitas. He often presided over the 11 AM high mass. Children normally went to the 9 AM mass. But I instead would sometimes attend the seemingly endless rituals of high mass in order to listen to the inspiring choir of young women, some with trained operatic voices, singing beautifully from the upper loft, filling the church with rapturous hymns. *Ave Maria!*

Then Monsignor Archese would give his sermon in Italian, sometimes repeating some of the same points in English for the benefit of those who had only an elusive command of the mother tongue. I remember on one occasion he was saying (in English) that it was our duty to be good. "If I'm good, you too can be good." He paused and then asked: "Why am I good?"

It was intended as a rhetorical question but I had never heard of rhetorical questions. As a child I was trained to give snappy answers to questions posed by adults. My hand shot up. I was sitting in the third or fourth row directly in front of the pulpit. Monsignor Archese looked down at me with incredulous eyes. No one in the audience ever dared speak at mass, least of all a child, and I was probably the only minor in the entire congregation. He pointed at me and said "Yes?"

I leaped to my feet and cried out: "You're good because you're a priest!" The entire congregation exploded with laughter. No one could quite believe this was happening, least of all Monsignor Archese who was trying hard not to look amused.

"Because I'm a priest? No, even a priest must let God into his heart. And that's how one is good; you let God into your heart." A good recovery by the monsignor. Then in a scolding but friendly tone: "And *you?* What are you doing here at high mass?" Another rhetorical question. This time I knew enough to remain silent, daring not to say "I just came for the music."

~ Final Decision ~

My mother grew mournful when she heard I was considering the priesthood. I was her only child, she reminded me. Who would feed her and support her and my father in their old age or take care of them if they got sick? Worse still: "If you become a priest, we'll lose you. We'll hardly ever see you." She began to cry. Moved by her tears, I immediately promised that I would never make that choice. Why enter the priesthood? You can't have a girlfriend or get married and you're always stuck in church, and worst of all, you might have to let your parents starve to death. The price seemed a little too high.

80

31/ *My First Protestant*

While still an altar boy, I had my first encounter with Protestant proselytizing. An evangelical preacher, tall, gaunt, and pale-skinned, was standing on the sidewalk on 118th Street not far from my house. By his side was a black valise with a small American flag sticking out from it. He held an opened Bible in his hand as he went on about the need to have "faith! faith! faith! in Jeeeuhsus! It's all here in the Holy Bible." He was the only Protestant preacher I ever recall seeing on the streets of Italian Harlem.

When he finished his sermon, the few curious people who had paused to listen drifted away. I approached him and told him I wanted to read his Bible. (I had noticed its splendid illustrations of dramatic biblical scenes.) He asked enthusiastically,

"Will you read this Bible if I give it to you?"

"Yes!" I exclaimed.

"God wrote this himself, son!"

"Wonderful!" I had no idea God wrote books.

"Will you read God's words?"

"Yeah, sure!" By now we were both shouting with excitement.

"Then this good book is yours!" and he placed the Bible in my hands. When I started to thank him, he said, "Don't thank me, son; thank Jeeeuhsus!"

When I proudly showed the Bible to Father Mazziato and told him about the inflamed man on the street, he was less than enthusiastic. After thumbing through the book he told me to throw it in the garbage can because it was a *Protestant* Bible and Protestants only caused trouble for the Catholic Church and one's eternal soul.

In any case, we Catholics were never encouraged to give much attention to the Bible, not even the Catholic one. We were fed a passage or two of the New Testament during Sunday sermons and that was all. The Roman Catholic Church would bring us to salvation through its sacraments and sacred traditions. No need to puzzle or squabble over this or that biblical passage. No need for endlessly conflicting interpretations. The church had final authority over what to believe.

Many years later while writing a book about the abuses of theocratic religion (*God and His Demons*), I gave the King James Bible a careful reading. Put together by a Protestant *committee* in 1611, it is still the greatest of translations, having contributed so many undying expressions to our language. Yet I could not understand why Protestants placed such faith in a book that also was full of godly inspired brutalities, bloodletting, tribal aggrandizing, religious atrocities, deistic vanity, inanity and insanity. I now could see why the Catholic Church rationed out only a few carefully vetted gospel verses to us at Sunday mass.

Even today Catholic Bibles, of which there are a number of fine translations, are perforated with footnotes urging figurative rather than literal interpretations of some of the more improbable passages. I never heard a priest or nun claim that every word in the Bible was literally true, as I repeatedly heard from fundamentalist Protestant preachers.

As for the Protestant Bible that Father Mazziato denounced, instead of discarding it I took it home, and for several nights I thumbed through it. I could not grasp much of what I read but I enjoyed the realistically painted and highly dramatic illustrations. But no matter what I gleaned from its pages, I continued to feel uncomfortable because it was a *Protestant* Bible. So one morning on my way to school I tossed the beautifully bound and finely illustrated book into a garbage can just as my priest had told me to do.

By the age of fifteen I drifted away from the church. I still occasionally attended mass on Sunday but it was now mainly to associate with my pals and flirt with the girls. Church was a place to see and be seen in your Sunday best.

When I was seventeen, while still feeling the grief of my mother's death, I decided to try to reactivate my religious devotion. I went to Holy Rosary Church one Saturday eve to make a confession, the first in quite some time. It was getting rather late. As I knelt in the pew saying my penance, I could hear the priest impatiently jiggling his keys. "C'mon now finish up, boys" he called to me and one other penitent. He wanted to lock up. From the basement below, I could hear the church bazaar going full force. An amplified voice was saying: *"Place your bets, ladies and gentlemen, place your bets."* Then the spin of the roulette wheel.

As I hurriedly rose to leave, the priest said, "Don't forget to go down to the bazaar and play some of the games." He gave a nervous laugh, maybe because of the angry look I gave him. I left the church and never returned, never to place bets on my immortal soul.

~ From Bells and Candles to Books ~

I still like to visit Catholic churches now and then, especially when in Europe. But in my salad days in East Harlem it was the local library that became my oasis and sanctuary. The library was a socialist institution, although I did not know it then. It served communally on a nonprofit basis, being publicly funded. Books were available for everyone to read at no cost. When I got tired of hanging around the handball court or the poolroom or the street, I would go to the library where I devoured numerous books not because I had some high-flown devotion to knowledge and intellectuality but because books offered passage into other worlds, other realities and experiences yet to come.

Yesterday's neighborhood library was far more nourishing to my mind and spirit than the neighborhood church.

As the years went on I became increasingly critical of religion. I could not help notice the venality, hypocrisy, material greed, pretense, intolerance, reactionism, and dogmatism that characterized so much of organized religions. I could not overlook the exploitative collusion between worldly wealth and heavenly worship. I now look back on my early years as a religious believer as a time that could have been better spent free from worries about sin and hellfire.

Eventually liberation theology came along to give a social dimension to virtue and salvation, to challenge the terrible wrongs perpetrated upon vulnerable populations in Latin America and elsewhere by the rapacious plutocracy. Now virtue was something more than merely a matter of personal piety and abstinence. Virtue meant fighting for social justice, building a kinder and more humane society out in the real world.

But whatever new breath was injected into the old religion by liberation theology, it did not matter to me. *Aggiornamento* was fine, and I rooted for a liberated revitalized church that sided with the oppressed against the oppressors. But I personally no longer believed any of it, neither the theology, nor the thundering godhead, nor the threat of eternal hellfire, nor the magical sacraments, nor the fabled Bible, nor the loving saints and furious holy spirits, nor certainly the duplicitous and venal men who held sway.

When the Vatican political reactionaries came roaring back into power, led by Pope John Paul II, it was clear that the old hypocrisies, criminal abuses, cover-ups, social injustice, perdition and predation were once more the order of the day.[8] If theirs was the road to heaven, who needed hell?

৪৩

32/ *Someone Else To Remember*

My junior high school was housed in the same building as Benjamin Franklin High School, whose student body in those days

---

[8] For further discussion, see my *God and His Demons* (Prometheus, 2010) 129-133.

was mostly Italian American. Both the junior and senior high schools were all boys.

The high school principal was the noted educator-scholar Dr. Leonard Covello, a man who wanted to see Italian kids excel not just so they might enjoy upward mobility and advance their personal fortunes. He wanted them also to make some kind of contribution to the community. Such was the case with Covello's own career, an upwardly mobile educator but also a community leader wielding a downtown influence on behalf of East Harlem. One of Covello's goals was to see that the various ethnic groups (Italians, Blacks, Irish, Puerto Ricans) learned to live in peace with each other.

One of his protégés was Vito Marcantonio, who much fulfilled the Covello model of selective acculturation into the wider society: impressive upward mobility with much personal accomplishment, yet retaining a strong attachment to his ethnic community roots.

Marcantonio represented the 18th Congressional District (mostly East Harlem) in the U.S. House of Representatives. Among all the individuals ever to serve in Congress, Marcantonio took the most outspoken and persistently radical stances on behalf of working people, labor unions, ethnic minorities, world peace, public ownership, and social democracy. He could be judged also by the enemies he made: the moneyed interests, big landlords, corporations, fascists, militarists, imperialists, and reactionary witch-hunters.

Marcantonio's district was twice subjected to redistricting in the hope of defeating him at the polls. He had the audacity to join forces with the Communist Party on a number of issues and in various electoral struggles. For this he was Red-baited mercilessly by political opponents and the mainstream media. Under J. Edgar Hoover, the FBI amassed a huge file on Marcantonio and deliberated every year about putting him on the Security Index for detention in time of emergency.

Marc (as his supporters called him) contested nine Congressional elections over the years, of which he won seven. In his last try for re-election in 1950, the Republican, Democratic, and Liberal parties joined together to back one candidate, a Republican named Donovan who lived downtown, outside the 18th Congressional district on swanky East 58th Street. Running on the American Labor Party ticket, Marc still carried Italian Harlem but lost to what he rightly called the "gang-up." I remember the sympathy we all felt for him at the time. In his excellent biography of Marcantonio, Gerald Meyer observes: "There is something distasteful and disquieting in the amount of power that was amassed to silence the only opposing voice in Congress."[9]

In my earliest years I was suspicious of Marcantonio, fearing that he might indeed be a Communist. My father saw him as "a man of the people" who helped anyone who came to his office including many who do not live in his district. This was quite true and quite impressive. It certainly was enough to win Poppa's vote. By the time I got to college my politics had awakened sufficiently for me to become a Marcantonio supporter.

Marc was born in East Harlem and lived all his life within a few blocks radius. He was a short man of slight build. His voice and diction carried a New York street nasality. Yet the fire and the content of his remarks were compelling.

Late one night (when I was about 14 years old) I chanced upon a big rally being conducted at what was known as Marc's "Lucky Corner," on 116th Street and Lexington Avenue. Given the hour and the venue, the crowd of five hundred or more consisted almost entirely of men drawn from the surrounding Italian neighborhood. Several speakers addressed the crowd, each telling a story of how

---

[9] Gerald Meyer, *Vito Marcantonio: Radical Politician, 1902-1954* (State University of New York Press, 1989) 6.

Marc had fought for some cause that directly helped them and others.

Finally, Marcantonio himself took the microphone and launched into one of his fiery speeches with deadly seriousness and scornful humor, striking blows at those atop the social pyramid. (I recall thinking to myself that someday I might be addressing large audiences.)

In the middle of Marc's speech something most unusual happened. A caravan of cars—shooting sparklers, flashing bright lights, blasting melodious horns and wild music, and sending balloons aloft—came rolling up Lexington Avenue from Spanish Harlem right alongside the large crowd gathered on 116th Street. It was a Puerto Rican invasion!

Feelings between the Puerto Rican and Italian communities at that time were strained, as is often the case when low-income ethnic enclaves find themselves competing for housing, schools, and recreational areas. The Italians saw the Puerto Ricans as encroaching; the Puerto Ricans saw the Italians as shutting them out.

Now here they were, those wild Puerto Ricans rolling a blazing cavalcade right into the middle of Marc's talk and into the middle of Italian Harlem. Would he react with fury at the interruption? No, he flashed them a big smile, waived vigorously, and shouted an extended rousing welcome *in Spanish*. By now it was obvious that the invasion from Spanish Harlem was a friendly one. These were Marc's supporters and he had been expecting them all along.

What happened next was something I shall never forget. As if of one mind, the large crowd of Italian-American men all turned toward the caravan rolling up Lexington Avenue and broke into thunderous applause and deep-throated cheers. At that moment we realized that the Puerto Ricans were not our competitors; they were our allies. (In addition, we probably were impressed and proud that Marc could marshal such enthusiastic support from Spanish Harlem.)

Many politicians divide the common people against each other. Marcantonio brought them together, showing them their mutual interests—which was one of the reasons he was so hated by the powers that be.

~ Worst Side Story ~

The Puerto Ricans were looked down upon by many other denizens of New York City. They were latecomers of alien appearance, swarthy, smallish, poor, speaking machine-gun bursts of Caribbean Spanish. They washed the dishes in the luncheonette kitchens, pushed the carts in the garment district, and toiled over noisy machines in light industry factories.

What struck me about the Puerto Ricans I got to know or had casual exchanges with was their warm and kindly contact. They seemed like the nicest people one could encounter. My friend, the noted chemist and spectroscopist, John Rocco Lombardi once said, "It's a myth that New Yorkers are unfriendly. There are so many good-natured friendly New Yorkers." "You mean the Puerto Ricans, don't you?" I said. "Well, yeah," he answered, "Puerto Ricans and maybe some other Latinos."

The Puerto Rican population of East Harlem in the late 1940s largely supported Vito Marcantonio because he was on the side of the renters and workers, not the landlords and bosses. He fought for the inclusion of Puerto Rico in the 1939 extension of the Social Security Act. He fought for job programs for Puerto Rican immigrants, and for a minimum hourly wage in Puerto Rico and numerous other legislation for the island's inhabitants. In his first House speech in 1936, he declared: "Puerto Rico is the most tragic victim of American imperialism."[10]

People loved Marc because he meant it. He also lived it. He worked tirelessly building an effective organization that was both a political machine and a social service agency. His office in East

---

[10] See Meyer, *Vito Marcantonio*, chapter 7.

Harlem was always open to people in need. He put in 14-hour days and never took a real vacation throughout his public career. In 1954, at the age of 52, he burned out; while getting ready to launch a campaign for mayor, he fell dead in the street.

I went to his funeral, waiting in the long line to pass his open casket. Then out in the street again I found myself in conversation with a saddened African-American woman. She told me how much inspiration and clarity Marc had brought to everything and how she would miss him. We both missed him already.

Vito Marcantonio goes unnoticed in the official political history of this nation. But he was loved and mourned by hundreds of thousands. For some of us he remains unmatched.

And I will never forget that night on Lucky Corner when that entire crowd of Italian men did a left face toward Lexington Avenue and gave heartfelt cheers and applause to their newly acquired Puerto Rican allies, just as Marc wanted.

~ *Part 7: Benito and the Old Country* ~

33/ *Living with Mussolini*

For many of the old Italian immigrants, Benito Mussolini appeared on the world stage in 1922 as something of a redeemer. Through his exploits in Africa and by "standing up" to other European powers, Mussolini won "respect" for Italy and for Italians everywhere—or so many of the immigrants imagined.

From the outset Mussolini was hailed and boosted by U.S. financial and industrial leaders and media moguls. The American upper crust openly adored him. Cole Porter waxed lyrical in one song: "You're the tops, you're the Mussolini" (lyrics he later deleted). *Il Duce* supposedly was the strongman who "made the trains run on time" (the trains were already running on time under the liberal constitutional monarchy that preceded fascism). It was he who crushed the Communists and Socialists, a "fine fellow" who "whipped the country back into shape."

Not enough good things could be said about Mussolini in the American press in the 1920s. Pick up the 5 May 1928 issue of the *Saturday Evening Post*; just under the Norman Rockwell cover, instead of the usual list of contributing authors, the entire space is taken up in large print with: "Beginning a Series of Personal Memoirs by BENITO MUSSOLINI."

"When Mussolini came along," an elderly Italian once told me, "they stopped calling us 'wop.'" The statement was woefully inaccurate. The unrestrained admiration expressed for Mussolini by the affluent class in America and its mainstream press did not at all generate a new respect for Italian immigrants. If anything it bespoke a low regard for them. U.S. plutocrats thought no better of ordinary Italian workers than they did of their own American workers. If anything, they saw the Italian as a vice-ridden ne'er-do-well, a disorderly bumpkin lacking the proper Calvinist virtues, just the sort of person most in need of a dictator's firm hand.

The second generation, that is, the children of the immigrants, usually spoke of Mussolini with derision, especially after the United States entered World War II. I recall occasional arguments in my grandfather's house between the older and younger men. (With one or two exceptions, the women were less likely to voice opinions on such matters.) As the war progressed and Mussolini showed himself to be nothing more than Hitler's acolyte, the old men tended to grow silent about him. But in their hearts, I suspect, many of them never bore him much ill-feeling.

For all the press attention accorded Mussolini over the years, too much was left unsaid. In his October 1935 speech, just before the invasion of Ethiopia, the dictator exclaimed, *"Italia proletaria e fascista, Italia . . . della Rivoluzione, in piedi!"* (Italy, proletarian and fascist, Italy . . . of the Revolution, arise!) These few words capture the immense class duplicity of fascism, propagated by fascist leaders in other countries as well, including of course Hitler in Germany. Pretending to be revolutionary and using a revolutionary idiom, they were in fact reactionary. Pretending to be for the common people, they served the corporate plutocracy, pursuing war and repressive power rather than peace and prosperity.

Proletaria? Rivoluzione? These leftist calls were designed to rally the masses around a retrograde revolution with a rightist outcome favoring the rich over the poor. To save themselves from the "fatal dangers" of communism, the people were to place their faith in *il Duce* and devote themselves to something new and daring—actually something that was derivative and falsely revolutionary.

Lofty proclamations aside, the fascists reduced the taxes and greatly increased the profits of the bankers, big investors, and industrialists who financed the fascist takeover. Throughout this "efficient" regime, corruption was rampant. At the same time fascist goon squads smashed the Italian proletariat's labor unions and newspapers, drastically increased the workers' taxes and cut their already low wages by half while lengthening the workday. Child labor was reintroduced and workplace safety regulations were trashed. Industrial abuses thought to have passed into history decades ago now reappeared.

~ The Alien Menace ~

Upon the United States' entry into World War II, about 112,000 Japanese, mostly U.S. citizens, were ruthlessly rounded up and incarcerated in detention camps for the duration of the war. Their homes, farms, and fishing boats were taken from them and they were consigned to economic ruination.

Less well known—and less severely treated—were the 1,600 Italian aliens who were arrested; 250 were interned in military camps for up to two years; and 600,000 others were forced to submit to curfews. Baseball star Joe DiMaggio's parents were classified as "enemy aliens." They had to carry photo ids; they lost their fishing boat (as did 1,400 other Italian-American fishermen), and were barred from San Francisco Bay.

Some 10,000 Italians were forced to vacate their homes in the restricted area along the west coast. Other Italians living near the coast were not allowed to own short-wave radios or flashlights.[11] The image was a terrifying one: little Luigi, up in his attic, using his flashlight to flick coded messages to a Japanese submarine, telling it when and how to attack the Golden Gate Bridge.

---

[11] See the writings of Lawrence Di Stasi and Stephen Fox. Fox reminds us that German "enemy aliens" were also interned.

In Mussolini's Italy, labor leaders, peasant leaders, and intellectuals were assassinated or beaten, tortured, and incarcerated under the harshest conditions. Such things—especially fascism's service to the superrich—went largely unreported in America (to this day). I have written about fascism's horrific human rights record, its oppression of the working class, its service to the wealthy cartels, and its wars of aggression.[12]

When Italy switched sides and joined the Allies in the last years of World War II, there was much relief and satisfaction among the American-born and probably even among many of the immigrants.

ଞ

34/ On the Trail of Benito's "Shadow"

On separate visits to Italy I had two passing "encounters" with Mussolini's shadow—so to speak. In the spring of 1952, when only eighteen years old, I was working as a courier at the United Nations Sixth General Assembly in Paris. After the job came to an end, I traveled for a few weeks to Florence, Venice, Rome, and Naples.

In Rome I made the acquaintance of two older lads who were lounging about the Piazza di Spagna with their girl friends. At one point they started talking to me about life under Mussolini. As adolescent schoolboys during the fascist era, they had been put into a youth organization. They would assemble in the Piazza Venezia to hear *il Duce* address the crowd from his balcony. Then the two of them, in self-mocking tones, repeated the chant they had mouthed as young blackshirts standing in the square looking up at Mussolini: *"Duce! Duce! Duce! Vogliamo la guerra! Vogliamo la guerra!"* ("Leader! Leader! Leader! We want war! We want war!)

---

[12] "Fascism, the Real Story," in *Contrary Notions: The Michael Parenti Reader* (City Lights, 2007), 341-352.

They shook their heads and grimaced. To them it now seemed so ridiculous, all that chanting for war.

It was an image I had often seen in old newsreels: Mussolini up on his balcony, strutting about with arms akimbo and chin jutting forward, a pompous, swaggering, tough-guy caricature of himself, the blood-drenched *buffone*.

My second encounter with Mussolini's "shadow" was closer to the mark. It came fifty-two years later in 2004. I was visiting a good friend of mine, Jerry Frescia, who lives in Mezzegra, an old hilly town perched on the shore of *Lago di Como* (Lake Como), the massive and magnificent body of water on the northern most border between Italy and Switzerland.

Jerry came from a New Jersey working-class, Italian-American family. He was (like me) a political scientist and a progressive political activist. He introduced himself to me at an American Political Science Association meeting in the United States in the 1970s and we became friends. Jerry was also a successful artist who sold his house in San Francisco, at a time when realty values were at a peak, and moved with his wife to Italy. From his rented villa on magnificent Lake Como he managed to glean some income by teaching art classes to Americans and other tourists who were spending time in Italy.

On the night of my arrival in Mezzegra, Jerry took me on a tour of the hilly town, with its old winding streets paved with large flat stones, lined with sturdy stone houses, archways, tiny courtyards, and all sorts of shrubbery. Like so many of Italy's villages, Mezzegra had aged ever more beautifully over the centuries. "Here in Mezzegra, Mussolini was caught and executed by the partisans," Jerry cheerfully announced to me. He pointed out the house where *il Duce* had been held prisoner the day before he was killed.

"Would you like to see where he was executed? There's a plaque to mark the spot." Yes, indeed. Suddenly I had an inspiration: "When we find the place he was shot I want to urinate on it." It would be my homage to Mussolini, a measure of his true worth. Jerry raised no objections to that plan.

After more uphill walking, we came upon a widening of the road and, to one side, a low wall not more than a few feet high. Fixed into the wall was a plaque made of the most beautiful ebony. Upon it was engraved the simple inscription: *"Benito Mussolini, 28 Aprile 1945,"* marking the time and place he was shot by an Italian partisan group.

I paused awhile, then walked up to the plaque and started to unzip, preparing to take my vengeance in hand, so to speak. Suddenly, I realized that I had no desire to do anything of the sort. In the still night and lamplight, amidst the village shrubs and ancient stones of the winding road, the beautiful ebony wood marked the exact place a human life, such as it was, had been taken. In life, a vicious pompous predator, spewing his grandiose rot in service to the plutocracy. Only in death did the aggrandizing fascist leader approach a certain humanity. The presence of death suddenly weighed upon me more heavily than the loathing I felt for the tyrant. So I refrained from watering Mussolini's shadow.

ॐ

35/ *How Italy "Won" World War I*

Everyone seems to agree that Italy was a pathetic joke in both World Wars. There was the story of how the entire Italian army landed one evening in Brooklyn to invade the Navy Yard, only to be routed and driven into the sea by the nightshift maintenance crew. Grandpa Giuseppe was not amused by such jokes. But they went on:

Did you hear that Italian battleships have their guns built on the sterns of their ships so they can fire while fleeing.

Do you know the battle cry of Italian troops as they charge into combat? "We surrender!"

When an Italian commander repeatedly called to his immobile troops: *"Avanti! Avanti"* (Forward!), one of them called out: *"Che bella voce."* (What a beautiful voice.)

The story goes that British leader Winston Churchill and Nazi leader Herman Goering were conferring about the impending threat of another world war. Goering leaned forward and said, "Don't forget, Mr. Churchill, this time we will have the Italians on *our* side." And Churchill chuckled, "That's only fair. We were stuck with them the last time."

The Churchill-Goering exchange is probably apocryphal but it shows how the image of Italian military cowardice goes back to the First World War, sealed in the popular imagination by the 1917 battle of *Caporetto*. In engagements leading up to Caporetto, the Austrian army had suffered 250,000 casualties and was on the verge of collapse. The Italians were making deep incursions into Austrian territory. The Germans could not afford to have their ally, Austria-Hungary, knocked out of the war. So they brought in a number of crack German divisions to join the fray.

The Italian divisions were now seriously outnumbered, in many instances poorly equipped, and—due to incompetent generalship—thinly fortified at their center defense line. In October 1917 the Austro-German forces launched a massive offensive; first, a gas attack that brought panic to Italian troops when they discovered that their defective gas masks offered little protection. Then a deadly accurate artillery bombardment followed by a massive frontal assault that broke the Italian center.

This was the battle of Caporetto. Half the Italian army was destroyed in what was one of the worst defeats in military history. I recall reading in a standard account of World War I that after Caporetto, Italy was no longer a factor to be reckoned with, having been essentially knocked out of the war.

Ernest Hemmingway made the disaster at Caporetto a focal point of his novel, *A Farewell to Arms.* In popular parlance, Caporetto became tantamount to Waterloo. Thus, someone who suffered a serious setback might be described as having "met his Caporetto." I don't think this phrase outlived the generation that actually remembered Caporetto—unlike "he met his Waterloo" which continues to enjoy currency two centuries after Waterloo. I suspect that Caporetto might today still retain passing mention in parlor conversations among those select cognoscenti who are still civilized enough to sip martinis and listen to Cole Porter tunes.

In any case, Caporetto was not the end of the story. The battered Italian army regrouped along the Piave and for weeks put up a stubborn resistance, repeatedly throwing back the fierce attacks launched by a much larger enemy force that was trying to finish them off. General von Dellmensingen, German chief of staff, later wrote that the Italians "can be rightly proud that they held" against "the best troops of both the Austro-Hungarian Army and their German comrades."

The story gets better; it begins to approach sanity, as wars seldom do. Now defending their own land, Italian troops seemed to recover their morale. They were promised by government officials that they could return to home and family if they just drove the enemy from Italian soil. Whether true or not, the presumed agenda was *fight for peace*—often the only thing worth fighting for.

Italian troops also became convinced that the Austro-Hungarian empire was tottering and that their counteroffensive along the Piave line would actually bring victory, peace, and an end to the entire Habsburg dynasty—one of those wildly delusional wartime scenarios that proved to be entirely correct.

According to one account, the resurgence of the Italian army and the home front after the Caporetto disaster was truly remarkable. The entire nation finally began to support the war effort. In a few months industry replaced all of the armament losses and munitions supplies. The army swiftly recovered its strength. "Measures were taken to minister to the physical needs and restore the battered morale of the Italian soldier. . . . New organizational methods for defense and offense were developed which sought maximum results with a minimum loss of life."[13]

The first imperative of any soldier—according to the cant mouthed by war leaders and super patriots—is to fight with uncompromising valor and with a readiness to sacrifice one's life for one's country. In truth, the first and sometimes only desire of almost every soldier in every army is to stay alive and get home in one piece, the exact opposite of fearless heroism.

But there actually are moments or situations in which warriors transcend the constricting impulse of self-preservation. In the heat of battle they come out of themselves. Sensing victory, they fight with a resolve and fury that helps to swing the tide their way. This seems to be what happened to the Italian army.

The war ended with the eleven-day battle of Vittorio Veneto and the complete defeat of Austrian and German forces by the advancing Italian divisions. Italy actually won the war on the Austro-Hungarian front. Yet most of my life I had heard how the cowardly Italians were smashed at Caporetto never to recover. Interesting how certain historical images and vignettes assume invincible fabrication.

The Italian contribution to the Allied cause in the First World War went further. An Italian army was sent to the Western front, where it performed with distinction against German troops in the victorious Second Battle of the Marne. Italian divisions also fought in Macedonia and Albania. All together, some 650,000 Italian troops were killed in action and a million more were seriously wounded or maimed.[14]

---

[13] http://www.ww1-world-war-one.info/WWI-Information-Italian-Front-Battle-Caporetto.htm.

[14] http://www.ww1-world-war-one.info/WWI-Information-Italian-Front-General-Commentary.htm.

All this heroism and terrible sacrifice on the altar of war is really nothing to be very proud of. I dwell on it only to show that the Italians do not deserve the historical reputation of mass cowardice so frequently accorded to them. Italy's performance in World War I was nothing to be ashamed of. But as with most wars, it also was a horror.

ଚ

36/ How Italy Also "Won" World War II

There were other "victories" that Italian forces secured, such as: the invasion of Libya in 1911 and the subsequent bloody occupation and pacification of that country; the invasion of Ethiopia in 1935-1936; the use of Italian fascist forces against the Spanish Republic in 1936-1939, and other attacks against weaker unoffending nations—undertakings that are shameful and disgraceful blots upon Italy's proud history.

In the Second World War (1939-1945) fascist Italy, joined with Nazi Germany in a war of aggression, suffered a number of staggering military defeats, most notably against the Greeks. The military performance of Italy's legions in World War II proved to be a serious embarrassment to those who had been anticipating Mussolini's version of the Second Coming of the Roman Empire. The ordinary recruits in the Italian army had no desire to get themselves killed in *il Duce's* wars. Their readiness to surrender and unwillingness to give their all on behalf of Nazi and fascist conquest should be a point of pride rather than a cause for derision. I feel only pride that so many Italians did not want to die for Benito, let alone Adolf. And I feel only disgust for the ones who willingly supported fascism's wars of aggression.

In no other country did so much of the population "lack confidence in their government so early in the war as in fascist Italy," writes one historian. The Italians could not see what was to be gained from this enormous and costly venture. "Mussolini himself frequently lamented the party's inability to create a fascist consciousness in the majority of Italians."[15]

Furthermore, there are parts of this story that deserve a better telling. The Italian army *did* distinguish itself in World War II in a remarkable way that has remained largely uncelebrated. In Southern France, and in Greece, Croatia, and some other areas in Eastern Europe, Italian military personnel—very much on their own initiative and with no support from the Vatican—refused to cooperate in the mass roundups and extermination of Jews, and instead gave sanctuary to considerable numbers of potential Holocaust victims.

There is no need to portray the Italians as pure and faultless. With the 1938 alliance between fascist Italy and Nazi Germany, laws against Jews within fascist Italy were passed. Twenty-five Jewish-Italian generals and admirals were abruptly dismissed. Italian Jews were forced out of university positions. Working-class Jews suffered employment discrimination. Foreign Jews in Italy were deported. There were no mass killings but the sanctions imposed on Italian Jews, especially those of low income, were severe at times.

But elsewhere in Europe the Italian military never got with the plan for a final solution. In Croatia, which was divided into German and Italian occupied zones, the Ustasha (Croatian Nazis) were given a free hand to rampage through the German zone, destroying entire villages and slaughtering tens of thousands of Serbs, along with lesser numbers of Jews and Roma ("gypsies").

These massacres prompted a furious response from many Italian army officers and enlisted men who refused to cooperate in exterminating innocent civilians. Instead, on their own initiative, they gathered up Jews and Serbs and moved them to protected

---

[15] Edward R. Tannenbaum, *The Fascist Experience: Italian Society and Culture, 1922-1945* (Basic Books, 1972) 308, 310.

108

areas. "Many lives were saved, and the infuriated Ustasha ceased operations in most of the Italian zone. Meanwhile, word spread and thousands of other Jews and Serbs fled from German to Italian territory."[16]

Another occupied country, Greece, was also divided into zones. In the German zone there ensued a roundup and deportation of Jews to extermination camps. Instead of following the Nazi example, the Italian military insisted that the Germans hand over all Jews of Italian origin. Italian consulate officials in the German zone proceeded to define "Italian" in the broadest conceivable way. As American historian Susan Zuccotti (Zuccotti is her married name; she's not Italian) reports, this included any Jew who had the remotest relationship to an Italian, Jews married to Italians, Jews married to Greeks, Jews with Italian sounding names. Often the Italians "demanded no pretext at all. . . . Italian military trains carried the released Jews to Athens, where they were fed, sheltered and protected."[17]

In France, in the territory ruled by the Vichy French (mostly Nazi collaborators) and German forces, the roundup and eventual extermination of Jews proceeded from late 1942 onward. But the Italian army ordered the Vichy French government to annul all arrests and incarcerations of Jews in the eight French departments that made up the Italian zone. In some instances Italian soldiers actually surrounded local prisons to insure that Jews held within would be released. The Italians refused to stamp "Jew" in anyone's identification papers or ration book. As in Croatia and Greece, word spread rapidly and thousands of Jewish refugees

---

[16] Susan Zuccotti, *The Italians and the Holocaust* (Basic Books, 1987) 76, and documentary sources cited therein. n.2, 296-297; also Barry M. Lituchy (ed.) *Jasenovac and the Holocaust in Yugoslavia* (Jasenovac Research Institute, 2006) xxxv.

[17] Zuccotti, *The Italians and the Holocaust*, 81.

fled to the Italian zone. This entire situation infuriated the Nazi leadership.[18]

Among the Nazi SS leaders (including Heydrich, Meuller, and Eichmann) who gathered at Wannsee in January 1942 to plan the final extermination of European Jewry, some complained of how uncooperative the Italians were in refusing to herd victims into the death camps of Europe.

It all began in the spring of 1941 when individual Italian army officers spontaneously refused to "stand by and watch Croatian butchers hack down Serbian and Jewish men, women and children." It ended in July 1943 with "a kind of national conspiracy to frustrate the much greater and more systematic brutality of the Nazi state," concludes Jonathan Steinberg after extensive research. The Italian resistance to the Holocaust "rested on certain assumptions about what being Italian meant."[19]

In Italy itself, thousands of Jews were given shelter not only by compassionate friends; "even government and police officials sometimes went against their own orders in hiding Jews, giving them false documents, and alerting them to the moves of the Nazi authorities."[20]

Here was courage and victory of a special sort, those moments *in extremis* when some people refuse to surrender their sanity and humanity. Italy went into World War II as a fascist puppet and came out with a record that contained some admirable accomplishments. That really is the only way to win—or lose—a war.

---

[18] Zuccotti, *The Italians and the Holocaust*, 83-85.
[19] Steinberg cited in John Cornwell, *Hitler's Pope* (Penguin, 1999) 254-255.
[20] Tannenbaum, *The Fascist Experience*, 317.

~ *Part 8: Moving Along* ~

37/*Outrunning the Dogs*

As much as I loved my extended family, I still longed for experiences beyond East Harlem. There were several cousins with whom I was especially close who read books and shared ideas and experiences about the wider world.

In my later years I was often asked, what inspired me to transcend my poor working-class background, go to college, get a Ph.D. at Yale University, and become an author, scholar, and political activist. My answer, in a word, was "dogs."

My grandfather had a brown dog whom he named Brownie. An uncle had a white dog whom he named Whitey. My parents became owners of a spotted dog whom they named Spotty.

Such was the level of imagination in my family. I knew then that I had to go forth and get an education and learn about other realms—and certainly at least learn more inventive names for pets.

In the course of my excursions into the world beyond, I suffered some of the hidden injuries of class. The marks of my unpolished origins were evident in my physical appearance and speech patterns. On one occasion I and my parents were visiting cousins who lived in a middle-class (non-Italian) neighborhood in the Bronx. While playing with one of my cousins and some other youths on the street, and forgetting that I was not in East Harlem, I called out "T'row da ball!" One older blonde girl grinned at me. "T'row da' ball! T'row da ball!" she called out, her taunting voice dripping with amusement. Other kids took up the mocking cry.

In East Harlem I would have just responded with my rapier wit: "Go fuck yourselves!" But here I was out of my element. So I just grit my teeth and continued to play in silence, retiring from the game at the first opportunity.

> **~ Running Away From Home ~**
> Departing from the family is not always an easy thing. It varies with ethno-class backgrounds. I recall talking with two friends of mine in the late 1970s. One of them, Bill Cartwright, came from an upper crust Nordic-Protestant background: Choate, Amherst College, Harvard Law. He said that when he announced he was leaving home, his affluent father gave him a wad of money, a pat on the back, and wished him luck.
>
> That was quite different from my experience, as I told my two friends. When I informed my working-class Italian father I was leaving, he threatened to kill me. "You can't shame the family! You can't abandon the family!" he thundered. I was quite shaken. In any case, I did leave—only to a small apartment several blocks away still in the Bronx (I could not afford Manhattan), which eased my father's anguish and apparently left him feeling less homicidal.
>
> The third person in this exchange was my dear friend Howard Kahn who said: "When I announced to my Jewish father that I was leaving home, he threatened to kill himself. And then he had a nose bleed." It takes all kinds of stereotypes to build a great nation.

My accomplishments were not at all entirely mine. The "self-made man" is an iconic image in America. But I really cannot claim to be self-made. I was able to attend college only because the City College of New York (CCNY) was a tuition-free school. If I had been obliged to incur heavy debts in order to pay thousands of dollars in tuition, as demanded these days by public institutions as well as private ones, I could never have continued my education. So I am greatly indebted to progressive individuals of generations before, whose names I do not even know, who fought for the principle of free higher education, the idea that a worker's child can get a degree and venture into reserves that are usually open only to the offspring of affluent families.

As it was, when I graduated high school in 1950 I did not go straight to college because I had to work. My mother was dying; medical bills were high; and my father's earnings were low. (We had never heard of medical insurance.)

Two years later, after working at the United Nations messenger department in New York and later on in Paris at the United Nations Sixth General Assembly, I returned home and started my studies at CCNY. I did four years of undergraduate work in three years, carrying an extra heavy course load. At the same time, I worked fifteen hours a week in order to earn enough money for my books, clothes, lunch, and car fare, while I lived in the Bronx with my father, step-mother, and her two children.

After City College, I won a teaching fellowship to Brown University where I taught for two years while getting a master's degree. Then I was awarded a stipend that enabled me to go to Yale for my doctorate in political science. The Yale stipend program was built on the presumption that even people who are not affluent have a right to higher learning (at least a few of them do). So I worked hard and performed well but, again, like every other "self-made" person, I could not have done it had there not been many others before me who provided resources and channels that made it all possible.

It was at Brown University in 1955-1957, while studying for my master's degree, that I first experienced the affluent Nordic-Protestant Ivy League world that was so markedly different from my blue-collar Italian background. Brown was an education in itself: the creamy upper-class faces and crisp, self-assured diction, the tastefully understated garb, and other implicit distinctions that reflected the moneyed world from which these students came. Consider just their recreational skills: tennis, racquetball, skiing, bridge. What goes here? I asked myself. No handball, boxing, stickball, or pinochle?

But not every upper-crust student at Brown lived a life of champagne and orchids. I recall how one of my students came to my office and nervously requested that I assign him extra written work. "It's really important to be able to write well," he said with mournful urgency. I did give him extra writing assignments and went over them with him. It eventually came out that his father had been editor-in-chief of the *Brown Daily Herald*, had authored several books, and had repeatedly emphasized how important it was to be able to write well and make a successful career of it. He expected nothing less from his son. The poor brow-beaten kid spent many school hours nursing his writer's block.

A few weeks later, I encountered yet another student who suffered from a performance block because of a highly successful but overbearing father. The young man came to my office and asked me to please call on him in class. "It's really important to be able to speak before audiences," he said with a note of desperation in his voice. "Why don't you just raise your hand and I'll call on you?" I suggested. But he was unable to raise his hand. That was the problem. His father, a highly successful trial lawyer had constantly emphasized the utter importance of "the art of public speaking" brow-beating his son to the point of turning him into a semi-mute.

To avoid calling on him in class with a question not of his choosing, which could have led to a disastrous response or non-response, I worked out a system whereby he would grimace or bring his hand up slightly to his face or make eye contact, and I would take that as a signal. It seemed to work; on a number of occasions he was able to join the class discussion but only after I had called upon him, never himself volunteering. He once asked me how I was able to speak before all sorts of groups including unfriendly ones. I had no answer. I do know that if he had been

raised in an extended Italian working-class family, he we~~
had plenty of practice holding forth before both friendly and unfriendly audiences.

~ Italian Boy to Harvard? ~

Sometimes the educational channels do not facilitate achieve-
ment but discourage it. In the late 1970s, a friend of mine, Michael Calabrese, was strongly advised against applying to Harvard
by the career counselor at his Chicago high school. Michael's
grades were good. But as the counselor told him, "Harvard
doesn't take people like us." Michael was a good looking lad but
in a Mediterranean rather than Anglo-Nordic way. In any case,
the Chicago public high schools simply were not considered recruitment reserves for a place like Harvard.

So Michael prepared to go to the University of Illinois. But
another counselor came up to him and said: "Are you the kid who
edits the school paper? I heard what my colleague told you, but
there was another young man here many years ago who got a
scholarship to Harvard. You should apply."

Michael Calabrese did apply. He picked up two scholarships
and made it into Harvard. At Harvard, as he tells it, the Anglo
Protestants had their own exclusive circles as did the Jewish students. There were few Italians, so he socialized with the Black
students with whom he got along well. He went on to get a law
degree and a doctorate, while co-authoring a widely read, critical
study of the U.S. Congress.[21] Today Michael lives in Washington
D.C. with his Italian-American wife, and works for a think tank,
where he served as vice-president for ten years and is now a Senior Research Fellow.

It was then that I decided I was "fortunate" to have a father
who made it only to the fifth grade and never bore down upon me
with incapacitating performance demands. By the time I made it
into the sixth grade, I had surpassed him in education. Also, as a

---

[21] Mark Green and Michael Calabrese, *Who Rules Congress?* 3rd ed. (Bantam
Books, 1979).

truck driver and taxi driver, he did not pose any professional challenge to me—although now that I think of it, I am always a bit nervous when driving trucks, the few times I have done so.

80

38/ *Bread Story*

During World War II and afterward, my father drove a delivery truck for the Italian bakery owned by his uncle Torino. When Zi Torino returned to Italy in 1956, my father took over the entire business. The bread he made was the same bread that had been made for generations in Gravina (that town not far from Bari, Italy). After a whole day standing, it was fresh as ever, the crust having grown hard and crisp while the inside remained soft, solid, and moist. People used to say that our bread was a meal in itself.

The secret of the bread had been brought by my Zi Torino all the way from the Mediterranean to 112th Street in Manhattan, down into the tenement basement where he had installed wooden vats and tables. The bakers were two wiry Italian-American men, who rhythmically and endlessly pounded their powdery white hands into the dough, molding the bread with strength and finesse. Zi Torino and then my father after him, used time and care in preparing their bread, letting the dough sit and rise naturally, turning it over twice a night, using no chemicals and only the best quality unbleached flour. The bread was baked slowly and perfectly in an old brick oven built into the basement wall by Zi Torino in 1907, an oven that had secrets of its own.

Often during my college days, I would assist my father in loading up the bread truck at 5:00 AM on Saturday mornings. We delivered in the Bronx to Italian families whose appreciation for good bread was one of the satisfactions of our labor. My father's business remained small but steady. Customers, acquired slowly by word of mouth, remained with us forever. He would engage them in friendly conversations as he went along his route, taking nine hours to do seven hours of work. He could tell me more than I wanted to know about their family histories.

In time, some groceries, restaurants, and supermarkets started placing orders with us, causing us to expand our production. My father seemed pleased by the growth in his business. But after some months, one of his new clients, the Jerome Avenue Supermarket did the unexpected. The supermarket's manager informed my father that one of the big companies, Wonder Bread, was going into the "specialty line" and was offering to take over the Italian bread account.

As an inducement to the supermarket, Wonder Bread was promising a free introductory offer of two hundred loaves. With that peculiar kind of generosity often found in merchants and bosses, the supermarket manager offered to reject the bid and keep our account if only we would match Wonder Bread's offer at least in part, say a hundred loaves.

"Their bread is paper compared to mine," my father protested. Indeed, our joke was: the reason they call it Wonder Bread is because after tasting it, you wonder if it's bread. But his artisan's pride proved no match for the merchant's manipulations, and he agreed to deliver a hundred free loaves, twenty-five a day, in order to keep the supermarket account, all the while cursing the manager under his breath. In the business world, this arrangement is referred to as a "deal" or an "agreement." To us it seemed more like extortion.

In response to deals of this sort, my father developed certain tricks of his own. By artfully flashing his hands across the tops of the delivery boxes he would short count loaves right under the noses of the store managers, in the case of the Jerome Avenue Supermarket, even loaves that they finally started paying for again. "Five and five across, that's twenty-five, Pete," he would point out, when in fact it was only twenty-three. We would load 550 loaves for the morning run and he would sell 575 by legerdemain.

"Poppa," I said to him after one of his more daring performances, "You're becoming a thief."

"Kid," he said, "It's no sin to steal from them that steal from you." [*Individual competition in the pursuit of private gain brings out the best of our creative energies and thereby maximizes our productive contributions and advances the well being of the entire society.* Economics 101]

In the late-1950s I left home for a few years to go to Yale graduate school, only to return without a penny in my pocket. I asked my father to support me for a semester so I could finish writing my doctoral dissertation. In return, I offered to work a few days a week on the bread truck. My father agreed to this, but he wondered how he would explain to friends and neighbors that his son was 26 years old and still without full-time employment.

"Kid, how long can you keep going to school and what for?" he asked. "All those books," he would warn me, "are bad for your eyes and bad for your mind."

"Well," I said, "I'm getting a Ph.D." To this he made no response. So I put in a few days a week of hard labor on the truck. Nor did he complain. In fact, he needed the help and liked having me around (as he told my stepmother who told me).

When the bakers asked him how come, at the age of 26, I was working only part-time, he said: "He's getting a Ph.D." From then on they called me "professor," a term that was applied with playful sarcasm. It was their way of indicating that they were not as impressed with my intellectual prowess as others might be.

On the day my dissertation was accepted and I knew I was to receive my Ph.D., I proudly informed my father. He nodded and said, "That's good." Then he asked me if I wanted to become a full-time partner in the bread business working with him on the truck every day. With all the education out of the way, now maybe I would be ready to do some real work.

I almost said yes.

One day the health inspectors came by and insisted we could not leave the bread naked in stores in open display boxes, exposed to passers-by who might wish to touch or fondle the loaves with their germ-ridden fingers. No telling what kind of infected perverted predators might chance into a supermarket to fondle bread.

So my father and I were required to seal each loaf in a plastic bag, thus increasing our production costs, adding hours to our labor, and causing us to handle the bread twice as much with our germ-carrying fingers. But now it looked and tasted like modern bread because the bags kept the heat and moisture in, and the loaves would get gummy in their own humidity inside their antiseptic plastic skins instead of forming a crisp, tasty crust in the open air.

Then some of the bigger companies began in earnest to challenge our restaurant and store trade, underselling us with an inferior quality "Italian bread." At about this time the price of flour went up. Then the son of the landlord, from whom Zi Torino had first rented the bakery premises over a half century before, raised our rent substantially.

"When it rains it pours," my father said. So he tried to reduce costs by giving the dough more air and water and spending less time on the preparation. The bakers shook their heads and went on making the imitation product for the plastic bags.

"Poppa," I complained, "the bread doesn't taste as good as it used to. It's more like what the Americans make."

"What's the difference? They still eat it, don't they?" he said with a tight face.

But no matter what he did, things became more difficult. Some of our long-standing family customers complained about the change in the quality of the bread and began to drop their accounts. And a couple of the big stores decided it was more profitable to carry the commercial brands.

Not long after, my father disbanded the bakery and went to work driving a cab for one of the big taxi fleets in New York City. In all the years that followed, he never mentioned the bread business again.

ଛ

39/ *Tony Faces the Irish*

My first really serious girlfriend was Mary O'Rourke. We got together when I was starting college in 1952 and Mary was studying to become a nurse. Mary's parents were prototypes of the hard, flinty, working-class Irish-Americans of New York. They made it clear to her that they were not happy with her dating an Italian boy. Even though they knew my name was Michael, they repeatedly referred to me as "Tony" (so Mary informed me). "Going out with Tony again, are you?" they would say to her.

Mary and I eventually got engaged. In time, her parents accepted the idea that Tony might become their son-in-law. To their credit and Mary's relief, they seemed to soften up to me. But I suspected that the O'Rourkes still prayed for a post-Tony era.

To their horror they got it. Eventually Mary and I broke the engagement. Then she met and married a *Jewish* engineer-salesman. Tony was bad enough, but now heaven itself came crashing down, a deluge of angry shamrocks—badda bing, badda boom—burying alive a nice Jewish boy. Mary's parents refused to attend her wedding. They never spoke to her again.

Mary's parents aside, the Irish had come a long way by the 1950s. A century earlier, they had arrived on these shores penniless, in great numbers jammed into the urban slums, with a reputation for alcohol-driven pugnacity. They were said to be shiftless, conniving, unclean, clannish, sodden, and riotous—the same litany of unappetizing attributes tagged onto other groups such as Native Americans, Blacks, Italians, Poles, Jews, Chinese, and Latinos—give or take a few adjectives. In New England, the same kind of defamation was delivered upon the French Canadians who had migrated down from Quebec.

To this day many people still use the politically incorrect term "Paddy Wagon" to describe the police vans that are used to round up disorderly individuals. Paddy was—and still is—a nickname for "Irishman." Likewise "Hooligan," a good old Irish name, was made coterminous with hoodlum and violent ruffian, and has become a negative word in our vocabulary along with "hooliganism."

~ The Putrid Pecking Order ~

People from all sorts of ethnic backgrounds opposed inter-ethnic marriage in the 1950s. My Aunt Lucy (my mother's sister), a woman of vitriolic tongue and aggrandizing demeanor, went on the warpath against her daughter, my Cousin Jay, whom I loved dearly. Jay had decided she was going to marry a young man who was Polish-American. Aunt Lucy believed that marrying a "polack" was marrying down, for Poles were of low reputation and they allegedly drank heavily. But worst of all, they were not Italian.

I had no idea what to think about Polish Americans. With my parents I attended the wedding (Cousin Jay had prevailed). Jay's newly acquired Polish in-laws, knew how to keep a party going. They danced the Polka with splendid foot-stamping aplomb. I also found myself admiring the tallish, blondish, solidly-built, Polish women. What is there not to like about polacks? I wondered. "They're Catholics, aren't they?" I asked my notoriously anti-Semitic Aunt Lucy. "Well, yes, they're Catholic," she grudgingly allowed. No matter. She sat frowning through the wedding festivities. One thing we can say about ethnic enmity: it never seems to be in short supply.

What the small-town Protestant bigots found hardest to swallow was the fact that the Irish were *Roman Catholic*. Worse than their poverty was their popery. But by the 1930s or so, the Irish had turned much of this around. They had became America's most popular ethnic group, according to some commentators.

There were the Pat and Mike Vaudeville comedians, traditional Irish music, and sentimental ballads. Then there was that truly great singer-dancer-actor-composer-lyricist-producer, George M. Cohan (an Irish Catholic); also the legendary Fighting 69th Regiment of World War I composed entirely of New York boys, mostly Irish; the Hollywood films with Pat O'Brien, Jimmy Cagney, Barry Fitzgerald, and many other favorites who gave us the prototypic Irish cop, priest, gangster, politico, and song-and-dance man.

But for me and a lot of my Italian-American friends, the Irish were a real challenge. Well into the 1940s and 1950s, in New York and other Northeastern cities, the Italians found themselves up against the Irish in the police and fire departments, Catholic schools and clergy, Democratic Party organizations, construction trades, labor unions, and postal and municipal services. One exception was the Sanitation Department. As early as the 1930s, the Italians found job opportunities doing the dirtiest work: collecting garbage. They dominated the New York Sanitation Department.

A second-generation Italian-American detective in the New York Police Department, whom I interviewed for a study I did at Yale back in the late 1950s, spoke with great bitterness about the years of discrimination he endured:

> I was the first Italian and I was resented by all the other [detectives]. They'd say, 'Hey, how did you get over here, you're an Italian'. . . . Twenty-two citations and I never made first grade detective, while fellows I broke in, in five years made first grade . . . . I was broken hearted.
>
> They being of different nationalities, Irish and German in particular, they tried to take all the credit. I broke in three or four other Italian fellows there. They're the same as me, hardworking family men. But no promotions for them. . . . I worked hard,

sometimes fifteen hours a day, two gun battles, wounded once but no promotion to first grade.

Those old-time Americans think they own the city of New York. . . . In their off-hand way, they are always ready to say, 'that guinea' or 'that wop.' They always think they're better than the average Italian American or Jewish American. They always have that chip on their shoulder that they were born here and are supposed to be better than us or the Jew. But unknown to them, they immigrated here the same as the rest of us.[22]

This bitter testimony was recorded over half a century ago. Relations among the various White ethnics, though far from perfect, have vastly improved since then.

The Italian Americans were largely an urban people often caught in an urban crisis, trying to maintain neighborhoods not out of some lofty commitment to preserve "earthy colorful communities" but out of economic necessity. Along with other modest-income ethnic groups they were forced to give way to the developers' expansionist plans. Arson (by the developers) proved to be an efficient way of "cleansing" blue collar neighborhoods for the benefit of profiteering investors. For awhile arson was the fastest growing crime in America, the meanest mode of gentrification.

But from the 1960s onward, the Italians were moving upward, much as the Irish before them. Many Italians made it into suburbia. Throughout the northeast, Italians now dominated the construction workforce. Substantial numbers gained employment in the various fire departments and the U.S. postal service, and in various labor unions. By the 1970s and 1980s, in police departments located in various northeast cities, the Italians gained top

---

[22] Michael Parenti, *Ethnic and Political Attitudes: A Depth Study of Italian-Americans,* (Ph.D. Dissertation, Yale University, 1962; reprint edition, Arno Press, 1975) 49, 85-86.

leadership positions, sometimes with deliberate design vengefully overthrowing a longstanding Irish dominance.

Italians produced numerous municipal political leaders, including the most prominent Tammany Hall boss, Carmine De Sapio whose advance in his early days was resisted by the Irish Tammany chiefs who themselves were eventually unseated. Another sign of upward mobility was the way Italians were *departing* from the Sanitation Department, making room for African Americans who, as always, faced the worst prejudice and were consigned to the toughest dirtiest jobs at the back of the ethnic line.

As with the Irish before them, the Italians found celebrity and Americanization in popular culture and music. A whole generation of crooners achieved stardom, including Russ Columbo, Frank Sinatra, Perry Como, Frankie Lane, and Tony Bennett. And by the late 1970s, Hollywood stars like Robert De Niro, Al Pacino, Sylvester Stallone, and John Travolta were shouting, shooting, punching, or dancing their way across the big screen.

In a word, the Italians overcame a lot of their marginalization and solved their "Irish problem" by taking much the same route as the Irish. And while the White ethnic groups melded into a more intermarried and less differentiated cohort, they still maintained oppressive attitudes toward African Americans and Latinos who were fighting their way up the greasy pole for better schools, jobs, and homes, while frequently enduring ethnic slurs and acts of harassment, brutality, injustice, and even murder by White ethnic police.

In my own personal experience I was made keenly aware of how Italians—rather than getting beat up by Irish cops—were now themselves becoming cops and doing some of the beating. In 1967, while back at Yale on a post-doctoral grant, I became very active in the anti-war movement. On one occasion, a group of us protestors tried to block the New Haven recruitment center. I was arrested for crossing the police line, then dragged backwards into the recruitment center and down the long corridor to be dumped into a police van waiting in the back lot.

One cop, an Irishman (not Irish-American but a relatively recent arrival from Ireland) with a florid complexion and thick brogue, had his arm locked around my neck and shoulder, all the while brandishing his club over my head and snarling in my ear, "I'll kill ya, ya dirrrty Communist bastarrrd!" Another cop was loosely holding me under my other shoulder; I could hardly see him. Following us down the hall was a third cop who kept slamming me in the stomach with his club.

Years earlier, when I was an undergraduate at City College, I occasionally used to spar and work out at the 23rd Street CCNY gym. We boxers would slam each other in the gut with a heavy medicine ball, back and forth, learning to take blows that "toughened" us. Now being dragged down the long hall, I tried to contract my stomach muscles as each blow hit me, just as I had learned to do at the gym.

The cop who was hitting me had the map of Italy all over his face, not to mention a name tag showing an Italian surname. Finally I said to him, "*basta, basta*" (enough, enough) in that age-old Southern Italian tone of entreatment not easily mimicked by the *americani*. He looked at me with wide-eyed surprise and immediately stopped hitting me.

There is something to be said for ethnic affinity.

&

40/ From Tammany to Television

My father was a *Mussoliniale*, I regret to say. He went to his grave without ever feeling too critical about the dictator. Poppa thought Mussolini got things done, organized society for the better, cracked down on crime and corruption, and created work opportunities. He had not the slightest information about the dictator's violent suppression of dissenters and was inclined to doubt such stories when I introduced him to them.

Most significantly, Poppa was convinced that *il Duce* had stood up to the French and British, the two powers that allegedly had stolen territory from Italy and acted like they owned the world. Taken together, the British and French imperialists—with their flags flying over sizeable chunks of the planet—indeed often did act as if they owned the world.

My father and I had words about Mussolini on several occasions. But in later years I injected a new modus operandi into my family visits: completely avoid all subjects about which we disagreed. This included, along with Mussolini, such topics as welfare programs for minorities, labor unions, and the death penalty.

Our conversations were best confined to the winning ways of the New York Yankees, news stories proving that politicians are crooks, favorable anecdotes about Italy and Italians, amusing family gossip, and various other human interest incidents. It was a source of satisfaction whenever I could introduce a topic that enlisted my father's appreciative attention.

On bread and butter issues, Poppa was not the worst. His loyalty was to Tammany Hall and the Democratic Party until the last decade of his life. He disliked Ronald Reagan's reign. As he put it, "That guy's good for only one group" (meaning big business). But in time, like so many other White ethnics, he felt betrayed by his party whose leaders, he believed, were giving "everything" to the Blacks and Puerto Ricans in the form of public housing and welfare—while the property taxes on his little house, jointly owned with his second wife (they lived in the Bronx), continued to swell.

"*We* [Italians] never were given welfare. *We* had to work for every penny. Why should they be living off me?" he would complain. When I reminded him that most of the people in poverty and on welfare were White not Black, he said furiously, "I don't give a damn what color they are. They should work for a living."

As taught by the powers that be, he believed that the poor were the authors of their own poverty. They were poor because they refused to work; and they refused to work because they were lazy.

The reactionary Republicans, with their usual resourcefulness, proffered a pseudo populism (still to this day) depicting themselves as protecting the "little man," the "middle American" from the "effete elite snobs," "the tax-and-spend Democrats," and "the special interests." While parading as champions of people like my father, they gave faithful service to the superrich at every possible turn.

The frightened and dim-witted Democratic leaders lost their way, wandering for forty years or so in that wilderness known as "identity politics," that is, race, gender, abortion, gay rights, lesbian rights, transgender rights, animal rights, prison reform, legalized drugs, and various other "life style" issues—all very good and important causes. But tireless emphasis on these "cultural issues," as they were called, worked to exclude a developed awareness of *class* politics, the unfair power and privileges of the wealthy, the growing gap between the superrich and the rest of us, and the increasingly serious bread and butter needs of the general populace. The plight of millions of working people like my father were left largely unattended, or so it was felt.

So Poppa, toward the end of his life, came to believe that his party had abandoned him in order to truck with more exotic constituencies. He also began to think the Democrats were "soft on crime." This itself is a story.

After years of toil my father looked forward to retirement time when he would be able to just "take it easy and enjoy life." Indeed, when he turned 65 he happily stopped working and started collecting Social Security, a modest amount supplemented by an occasional off-the-books job (such as driving a retired Judge Rosenthal somewhere every few weeks.)

Poppa seemed to enjoy the first few months of his retirement. In high spirits he would make toys for my stepmother's grandchildren in his basement workshop or repair something around the house. He planted a vegetable garden and occasionally accompanied my stepmother on errands. And he would watch television.

But a lifetime of hard work had left him with few opportunities to cultivate skills and interests that might have kept him satisfactorily engaged. After awhile he lapsed into a boredom and disappointment that he made no effort to disguise. "What about the senior center?" I suggested. "Aw, they're just a bunch of old fogies who get into arguments when they play cards," he responded.

All he had was television. He watched mostly crime shows which were available in superabundance. The more he watched, the more fearful he became of crime and the more readily he voted for politicians who claimed to be waging "a war on crime" and who supported the death penalty. In 1982, when Ed Koch, mayor of New York, an ultra-Zionist of crass politics and nasty disposition, ran in the Democratic gubernatorial primary against Lieutenant Governor Mario Cuomo (a more admirable person in my eyes), my father voted for Koch. When I asked him how he could choose Koch over Mario, he replied resolutely: "Cuomo's against the death penalty. Koch supports it."

At this time my father no longer lived in East Harlem (designated a high crime area). He resided in a North Bronx, Italian-American neighborhood, the kind that ethnic families move to years after their initial settlement (what ethnologists call a "second settlement area"). There was relatively little crime in the North Bronx, but Poppa's mind was living in Television Land where crooks and killers romped about without stint, leaving him more frightened about crime and "crime-ridden minorities," just as the right-wingers wanted.

~ Nobody Will Remember ~

When my father died in 1983, I lost not only him but all his history. There were things I now would never be able to ask him. I wanted to know where and how he learned to make homemade wine. How long had he worked at Johnny Mandy's Saloon as a bartender when I was very young? Did he get paid when he worked for the Tammany Hall Democratic Party machine getting out the vote? Where did he get the suicidal courage when he was 18 to buy a (stick shift) truck—and without a driver's license and without ever before getting behind a wheel in his life—drive it away bucking and kicking like a horse? Why was my middle name "John"? What drinking did he do during Prohibition and where? Where did he learn to dance so well?

Suddenly all these urgent questions came forward only to hang silently in the air, waiting for yesterday.

~ *Part 9: The Mess Media* ~

41/ *Italian Stereotypes*

The self images we Italian-Americans have embraced have not been of our own making. For the most part they were shaped by mass media forces beyond our control. This is true for just about every marginalized ethnic group in America. The commercially produced stereotypes are easily accepted by the entire society, including many members of the group itself.

In the 1970s, the media brought forth a new working-class Italian, "the Jivey Proletarian" as I called him in another work of mine[23] who was hip, streetwise, and neither a crook nor a cop, sometimes a comedy character like "the Fonz," unschooled—even if going to school, or the John Travolta character of *Saturday Night Fever* who crosses out of the Bay Ridge proletariat into a presumably better, finer, middle-class world in Manhattan.

By 2011, with the aid of such reality shows as *Jersey Shore*, the Italian-American proletarian came to be known as a *Guido*, with female counterparts designated as *Guidettes* (how utterly creative). Guido slurs his speech as he stumbles through his minimal vocabulary. He wears black T-shirts. He works out a lot, focusing adoringly on his abs. He is visceral, emotive, and spends his best waking hours "chasing chicks." The Guidette concentrates on doing her nails, adjusting her heaps of dark hair, and getting laid.

---

[23] Michael Parenti, *Make-Believe Media: The Politics of Entertainment* (Wadsworth/ St. Martins, 1992) 150ff.

It is a longstanding stereotype: the hot, not-very-classy, Italian female. For years the joke was:

Q. What do you do when an Italian girl wants to have sex with the lights on?

A. Open the car door.

Proletarian stereotypes have been not only of Italians but of other ethnic groups and of working-class people in general: loud-mouthed, unschooled, simple-minded, acting on impulse, living a life well worth escaping. The ethnic bigotry is also a class bigotry.

Not all generalizations made about ethnic groups are negative. Some actually can be complementary. Thus Italians are often seen as warm, outgoing, compassionate, musically gifted, of generous spirit, and dedicated to the family. Italian men have been described as devilishly attractive and superb lovers. There is not a single recorded instance of any Italian male challenging this stereotype. (And with good reason. Think for a moment about all the "strikingly handsome" Italians: Jimmy Durante, Alcide De Gasperi, Lou Costello, Leon Panetta, Al Capone, Joe Bonanno, Big Pauli Castellano, Savonarola, and others too good-looking to mention.)

Additional Italian-American stereotypes can be found in the world of television advertisements, as Marco Ciolli so well describes it: There is the Latin lover who wins his lady with his right choice of beverage; the Mafia don ready to start a gangland massacre if the lasagna isn't *magnifico*; the nearly inarticulate disco dimwit who can barely say "Trident" as he twirls his partners around the dance floor.[24]

Then there are the boisterous Italians vigorously shoveling platters of food around the table and into their mouths, resembling a rugby match with tomato sauce. The foodie stereotype continued into the twenty-first century. In 2006, a Pizza Hut television commercial featured an elderly Italian couple, dressed in the style

---

[24] Marco Ciolli, "Exploiting the Italian Image," *Attenzione*, September 1979.

of immigrants just getting off the boat in 1905. She exclaims "Oooh, mamma mia!" when the pizza appears, and he asks her in a scolding tone, "Why-uh you no make-uh pizza like-uh dat?"[25]

This is not to say that Italians are indifferent to their cuisine. As already recounted, our holiday dinners were sumptuous, lively events. Good food remains a precious part of the culture, just not the sum total.

~ Eat These Words, MacNeil ~

The linking of Italians with food is so predominant a stereotype as to preclude other associations (except, of course, organized crime). Thus a PBS mini-series on the English language, written and narrated by Robert MacNeil, dwelled at length on how various foreign languages have enriched the English language. However, Italian was something of an exception, MacNeil asserted, since the only Italian words he could find that have passed into English "all relate to food."

The food stereotype so pre-empted MacNeil's myopic vision as to cause him to overlook such inedibles as: *ghetto, umbrella, malaria, adagio, incognito, aggiornamento, agità, agitato, a capella, vendetta, obbligato, regatta, rotunda, imbroglio, vista, verismo, graffiti, allegro, bambino, baritone, basso, bravo, bravado, bravura, brio, buffo, bordello, libretto, tempo, cantata, cognoscenti, coloratura, contralto, crescendo, diminuendo, dilettante, diva, divertimento, falsetto, forte, fortissimo, fresco, illuminati, impasto, impresario, inamorato(a), inferno, intaglio, intermezzo, lingua franca, literati, maestro, operetta, ostinato(a), paparazzi, piano, piazza, pietà, politico, presto, prima donna, soprano, sotto voce, staccato, stiletto, studio, torso, tempo, vibrato, viola, virtuoso*—one could go on.

Ethnic stereotypy sometimes can predetermine who is and who is not designated an American. In my younger years I could not help being struck by the different treatments accorded Mother

---

[25] ABC-TV, Bay Area, California, 5 September 2006.

Cabrini and Lucky Luciano.

Cabrini was born in Lombardy, Italy, the daughter of rich farmers. She took religious vows at age 27 and soon after became Mother Superior of an orphanage. Her hope was to establish missions in China. But the Pope had other plans for this capable organizer. In 1889, on his instructions, Mother Cabrini was dispatched to New York City with six other nuns. In the years that followed, she set up Catholic orphanages in various U.S. cities and abroad. Cabrini died in 1917 and was canonized by the Roman Church in 1946.

What I remember of her canonization was the generous coverage in radio news reports, newspapers, and news "shorts" (customarily shown in movie theaters before the main feature, in the days before television). More times than I could count, Mother Cabrini was enthusiastically described in the media as "America's First Saint," and "the first American ever to be canonized." American? Even though I was just a junior-high schoolboy, I could not help noticing that no mention was ever made of Cabrini's thoroughly Italian antecedents.

Cabrini did not migrate to America until she was 39, and then only under the Pope's instructions. She finally became a U.S. citizen at age 59 and died at 67. In other words, she spent 59 years as an Italian and only the last eight years of her life as a naturalized U.S. citizen. Cabrini also was made patron saint of immigrants, an award that further acknowledged her own longstanding immigrant status. But the way the U.S. press played it, she was not an immigrant but a true-blue American who made us all feel proud to be Americans.

Now compare Mother Cabrini to Lucky Luciano who was, and still is, repeatedly described as an "Italian mobster."[26] Born in

---

[26] See for instance, "Lucky Luciano" from Wikipedia, the free encyclopedia, January 2012.

Sicily, Luciano migrated to New York City with his family when he was ten years old. He developed his criminal activities on the Lower East Side, not in Italy, and throughout the years he always thought of himself as an American.

According to one leading crime reporter, Luciano "was a brilliant criminal executive who created the framework, culture, and ground rules for the American Mafia 80 years ago."[27] Luciano also made use of Irish and Jewish mobsters to carry out crucial assassinations and other nefarious deeds. In 1946 (the very year Cabrini was being declared an American saint), federal authorities deported Luciano to "his native Italy," as the press repeatedly phrased it.

So there we have it. The admirable Cabrini who spent most of her life in Italy, was hailed as an all-American saint, while the loathsome Luciano, who lived in America from the age of ten and learned his vicious thuggery in this country, was repeatedly labeled an "Italian mobster" fit to be deported to "his native Italy." Such are the calibrated ways that saints and sinners reach their respective resting places.

&

42/ Gangsters and Banksters

Like many others who shared my ethnic heritage, I experienced some discomfort when, in 1951, Senator Estes Kefauver, a Democrat from Tennessee, launched his highly publicized investigation into the organized rackets, uncovering scores of thugs with Italian surnames. Subsequent decades produced an endless parade of such rogues whose faces were repeatedly splashed across the print and broadcast media.

I must admit that when it came to names, the mafia operatives really had them: *Scarface* Al Capone, *Lucky* Luciano, *Sammy the Bull* Gravano, *Joey Bananas* Bonanno, *Crazy Joey* Gallo, *Jimmy the*

---

[27] Selwyn Raab, Op-Ed, *New York Times*, 23 January 2011.

Weasel Fratianno, *Sonny Red* Indelicato, and *Sonny Black* Napolitano.

One could go on with *Joey Kneecap* Santorielli, *Johnny Bingo* Bosco, *Itchy Fingers* Zambino, *Big Paulie* Castellano, and *Lupo the Wolf* Saietta. Then there was *Johnny Blind Man* Biaggio, *Vinny Gorgeous* Basciano, *Cadillac Frank* Salemme, and *Fredo the Plumber* Giardino.

Finally, none of us will ever forget *Anthony Chicken Fucker* Bastoni (don't ask).

Listed in the crime reports was one Mafia boss from Philadelphia named Angelo Bruno. The name caught my eye. I knew something about him. Years earlier in Washington D.C., I had a conversation with a good friend of mine, Michael Maggio. Michael was a progressive, award-winning, nationally recognized lawyer, dedicated to fighting for social justice. He devoted much energy in struggling for the rights of immigrants who were fleeing from the US-sponsored counterinsurgency terrorism in Central America. Michael was a highly regarded humanitarian who stood up to the Washington autocrats. On one occasion he publicly compared the Immigration and Naturalization Service to "Dante's rings of hell."

In his youth, as a student at Temple University, Michael Maggio headed a radical group and later became a member of the Communist Party. As reported to me, Michael's father was glad his son had become a Communist because it kept him away from the hippie drug groups and the other weirdo counterculture things. By the time I knew Michael, he had left the party.

Along with being a fighter for the downtrodden and a genuinely nice person, Michael was one of the best Italian cooks I ever met. He could produce platters of the finest Southern Italian meals as *delizioso* as anything my grandmother or my father created, and he took great pleasure in doing so.

One day in the mid-1980s, as I sat with him in his Washington office, Michael Maggio revealed to me that Angelo Bruno, the noted Philadelphia mafia don, was his uncle. He went on to say that Mario Puzo, author of *The Godfather*, the best-selling novel that was made into a smash-hit movie by Francis Ford Coppola, had modeled his lead character Don Corleone after Angelo Bruno.

Michael claimed (accurately) that his Uncle Angelo had refused to deal in narcotics and sex trafficking, just like Don Corleone in the movie. Bruno also displayed an ability to keep the peace within the Philadelphia mafia. But because he would not let the Philadelphia mobsters enter the lucrative drug racket, he was shot dead by some of the hungry younger guns who wanted a piece of the action in narcotics.

"If there was ever such a thing as a nice mafia boss," Michael Maggio ventured, "it was my Uncle Angelo." Well, there is no such thing as a nice mafia boss once you look at their operations on the ground. Even if he eschewed narcotics and sex trafficking, Angelo Bruno was up to his ears in gambling, bootlegging, hijacking, loan sharking, and the like. He had a kindly side to his personality and he tried to keep the peace but when he had to come down hard, he did.

All this said, when Bruno was killed, the Philadelphia newspapers ran comments by readers who remembered him as the *capo* who kept the peace and kept narcotics out of most of Philadelphia.[28]

I recently discovered that Bruno's designated nickname in the official crime listings is *The Gentle Don*. Michael Maggio would have liked that. Too bad Michael is no longer with us. Although he kept himself in good shape, he tragically died in 2008 at the age of 60, at the height of his valiant but very taxing career as a fighter for friendless political refugees.

One might wish that the media gave more attention to the courageous struggles for social justice waged by Italian Americans

---

[28] Harry Costigan, letter to the *Philadelphia Inquirer*, 7 April 1980; see also Samuel P. Alfonsi, reminiscent piece on Bruno: "Shoeshine Boys Never Talked," *Philadelphia Evening Bulletin*, 31 March 1980.

like Michael Maggio, and a little less exposure to the mafia dons, be they "gentle" or not. Maybe Italian-American political activists should be given dashing names like Michael *The Magnificent* Maggio.

Let's go back to the aftermath of the Kefauver hearings. America, O America, God's glorious but ever besieged country, was in the grip of an organized crime network that threatened to destroy the very fabric of our society, or so we were repeatedly alerted. In fact, what the mafia bosses stole from the public was a pittance compared to the hundreds of billions of dollars that Corporate America regularly plunders from workers, consumers, small investors, and taxpayers. This went largely unnoticed in all the hoopla.

That Congress actually dared to confront the *mafiosi* was proof enough that these hoodlums were men of limited power. They did not sit on the governing boards of corporations, banks, investment firms, media networks, foundations, and universities as do the "captains of industry and finance." They could not buy Capitol Hill, the way the big corporations and their lobbyists have repeatedly done. Unlike the boardroom plunderers, the *mafiosi* did not occupy high positions in Washington or on Wall Street. They did not cavort with the top White House decision-makers and Pentagon contract fixers with their million-dollar kickbacks and mysterious billion-dollar budgetary evaporations.

The mafia dons did not relax or play golf with the paladins of wealth as did *Dirty Dickie* Cheney, or *Georgie the Blood Sucker* Bush, or *Slick Willie* Clinton, or Barack *Legs* Obama, or Bernie *Two-Faced* Madoff, or *Casino* Jack Abramoff, or Andy *Fasthands* Fastow, or Kenny *the Weasel* Lay. Now *that's* organized crime: the policymakers not the bookmakers, the banksters not the gangsters.

The uneducated mafia thugs seldom got close to the real money. If they had a corrupting influence on public officials, it was usually in limited and lowly spheres. Besides being small-time, these few hundred villains composed but a tiny sliver of an otherwise hardworking, law-abiding Italian-American population estimated at around twenty-four million, but this crucial datum continues to get lost in all the media hype.

෨

43/ "Ah Mafioso!"

There have been Jewish, Irish, Black, Latino, and even Anglo Protestant mobsters in our history. Today, we even see the emergence of Russian and Asian gangsters in the United States. None of these cutthroats are representative of the larger ethnic formations from which they happen to emerge. But it is the Italian crime syndicate upon whom the media have fixed. And not just the media. I have met progressive-minded people who would never utter a racist or anti-Semitic remark but who would make an Italian mafia joke right to my face and think they were being clever, not realizing they were being offensive.

Linking Italians as an entire group with criminal behavior has long been one of those "respectable" forms of bigotry, the expression of which can be found in high places as well as low. In the Oval Office tapes released during the Watergate investigation one can hear President Richard Nixon spewing these words to an assistant: "The Italians. We must not forget the Italians. . . . They're not like us. . . . They've never had the things we've had. Of course, the trouble is . . . you can't find one that's honest."[29] Such utterances from a man later driven from office for lying, cheating, and lawbreaking.

Another batch of Oval Office tapes released in December 2010, decades after Nixon's departure, offer more of his rancid opinions about ethnic groups. We hear Nixon underscore the genetic inferiority of Black people, telling us that if they were ever going

---

[29] Quoted in Garry Wills, "Nixon, Italian Style," *La Parola dal Popolo*, March/April 1975.

to catch up with the rest of the population, Blacks "have to be, frankly, inbred" (he must have meant "crossbred"). The Irish, Nixon insists, cannot hold their liquor; they get "mean" when they drink. And he returns once more to the Italians, this time deciding that they are "wonderful people," but their heads are not "screwed on tight."[30] Almost a compliment.

The stereotype of the Italian-American mobster is not only indelible, it is international. While I was in Lisbon during the revolutionary ferment of 1975, trying to get interviews with members of the Portuguese military for an article I was writing, I encountered an Army lieutenant who upon hearing my name asked me, "*italiano?*" No, I said, "*italiano-americano.*" To which he commented gleefully, "*Ah, mafioso!*"

A half-hour later the exact same inquiry and same response was smilingly accorded me by a Portuguese Army captain: "*italiano?*" "*No, italiano-americano.*" "*Ah, mafioso!*"[31] The lieutenant had right-wing sympathies, and the captain had leftist attachments—which demonstrates how Hollywood cuts its swath across the ideological spectrum.

~A Reader's Complaint~

"Why can't we Italians be known for Mario Savio, Carlo Tresca, Sacco and Vanzetti, and Fiorello LaGuardia?! Instead we have mafia thugs and Jersey Shore morons! In any other context, it would appear as the small minded bigotry it is!"
—Justin Addeo, email to me, January 2011

There is the case of Governor Mario Cuomo of New York, who decided against making a bid for the presidency in 1984 despite his popularity and national recognition. Cuomo, an outspoken

---

[30] *New York Times,* 19 December 2010.
[31] My companion on that trip, Cheryl Smalley, witnessed and can verify both of these seemingly scripted encounters.

liberal and gifted public speaker, would have needed to raise tens of millions of dollars to finance such a venture, and spend almost two years campaigning for the nomination and then the office. He never seemed willing to take it on.

I cannot count the number of individuals who in knowing tones concluded that Cuomo—a consistently honest public office-holder—very likely refused to make a bid for the presidency out of fear that *his past secret attachments to the mafia would be revealed.* This strange observation was voiced repeatedly like a mantra by all sorts of persons who had not a scrap of evidence or information pointing in that direction.

In fact, Cuomo's personal life had already undergone a fairly exacting vetting during his thirty years or more in public life—with no such mafia connection ever being unearthed. His ethnicity per se seemed to be taken as sufficient evidence that something was amiss.

Some years ago I was being interviewed for a teaching job at an east coast university. The interview was being conducted by the president and the dean of the school. The subject of ethnicity came up. The president, a Jewish American, proudly declared that Jews were the only ethnics in America who had produced a literature of their own. There was an awkward pause. The dean was African American. This was at a time when all sorts of gifted African Americans were writing novels, plays, poems, memoirs, exposés, social analyses, and political tracts. The president suddenly realized he had gone too far: "No, I mean Jews and Blacks. Yes, those are the only two groups that have produced a body of literature of their own."

It was my turn. I informed them that there was quite a substantial body of writings by Italian Americans but nobody seems to know about it because it is seldom distributed, reviewed, or treated in mainstream channels.

Ah yes, the Italians, chimed the president and the dean, suddenly keenly mindful of my ethnic background. The two of them then launched into a discussion about Italians, referring not to the rich historical and sociological literature by and about Italian Americans—about which they were completely ignorant—but to the movie *The Godfather*! In almost sentimental sing-song fashion, they went on about how closely knit was the gangster family, how they stuck together, and how important such loyalty was for the risky ventures they pursued.

~ Another Reader's Complaint ~

"What you write resonates painfully with my own experience growing up in one of the few Italian families at my elementary school, and in various workplaces where Italian references were laced with negative or demeaning stereotyping. Often the comments were said with a smirk or a chuckle. When confronted they just wouldn't accept that what they were saying was offensive. 'You're too thinned skinned,' I was told. And, those same people, well educated and moneyed, wouldn't dare these days make similar comments or assumptions out loud about Blacks or Hispanics. Though I'm pretty sure they had plenty to say in private.

"A few days ago I saw the actor Michael Douglas on TV talking about his recovery from cancer and how his wife was strong and supportive. He said, 'She's Welsh. Good thing. If I had married an Italian, she'd be shouting, Mamma, mia. Mamma mia.' He related this with a big grin and exaggerated hand gestures. "

~ Gary Gianini, email to me, January 2011

Uh no, I tried to say, excuse me but those are not the Italians I'm referring to. What about the noticeable numbers of Italian Americans who were now making contributions in government service, political life, sports, law enforcement, education, litera-ture, organized labor, the professions, entertainment, and the arts. For me the conversation was not making any sense. But the president and the dean persisted. Having seen *The Godfather*, they spoke with all the confidence of experts.

I found myself thinking that I might just slip out into the parking lot and slash their tires—if only to give some real-life confirmation to the pictures in their heads.

~ Part 10: Goodbye Italian Harlem ~

44/ Italy Discovers Pizza

In late 1951, at the age of eighteen, I quit my mailroom job at the United Nations Secretariat on 42nd Street on the promise that if I showed up in Paris for the United Nations General Assembly, I would be given employment. And so it happened. I worked as a *courrier diplomatique* (U.N. messenger). It allowed me to live in Paris, that magical city, for five months or so, enabling me to make some interesting friends, sit in the busy cafes, rent a little room in the *Quartier Latin*, and in my spare time feast upon the impressionist paintings at the Jeu de Paume and the art treasures of the Louvre and the Musée Rodin. After the U.N. General Assembly ended, I took what money I had and traveled to Florence, Venice, Rome, and Naples, to see the Old Country for myself. For some reason, I had no desire to visit Calabria or Bari, most likely because I had no surviving family connections there, and Italy for me had come to mean its legendary cities.

Florence had a neat and charming beauty. Venice was sweetly unreal, almost like a movie set. Naples was fecund and fetid, with more than a normal share of poverty and predators. It was in Naples that I first heard the Southern Italian speech intonations that were much like the ones heard in Italian Harlem, even though the latter were mostly in English.

In Florence I sat in the Medici Chapel for over an hour, keeping company with Michelangelo's brooding sculptures of Lorenzo di Medici and Giuliano di Medici, and the allegorical figures lounging at their feet. Then on to Rome to gape at Michelangelo's ceiling in the Sistine Chapel and his Last Judgment. I hungrily worked my way through the entire Vatican Museum. Rome was really the Eternal City with its priceless museums, churches, piazzas, and fountains.

One disappointment I encountered in Italy was the food. Especially in the northern cities of Florence and Venice, the restaurant meals seemed bland. I missed my rich Southern Italian home cooking.

There was not much, if any, pizza in northern and central Italy in 1952. Pizza was almost exclusively a Southern Italian dish. It also should be remembered that through the 1940s in the United States, pizza was a commodity sold only in Italian neighborhoods. In his 1942 study of the Italians of Newark, Charles Churchill informed his readers that Italian Americans ate something called *pizza*, carefully described by him as a "cylinder shaped" and "pie-like" flat crust covered with tomato sauce and cheese. He was opening up new culinary horizons for his American readers.

It was not until I got to Rome that I chanced upon an ice cream parlor, of all places, sporting a sign that read *"Pizza."* Pizzerias in East Harlem were filled with fragrant invitations of pepperoni, cheese, anchovies, tomato sauce, and olive oil, with a chef in full view inside the storefront window, flipping the pizza dough into the air in order to spin and stretch it. Bombarded with oven laced aromas, you had no doubt you were in a pizza parlor.

Now, in the ice cream parlor in Rome I skeptically inquired about the sign. The clerk assured me that pizza was available. He reached into the ice cream freezer and came up with a small flat frozen package whose contents he popped into a toaster and then served up to me. It was crisp with faint flavors of cheese and tomato on it. It wasn't bad but it wasn't pizza.

By the late 1950s pizza had become a mass-market, fast-food commodity in the United States but not so in Italy. Soon millions of American tourists were traveling to Italy repeatedly requesting pizza in restaurants. At the same time Southern Italians, who were migrating to northern Italy in search of jobs, also began to popularize pizza. Thanks to the tourists, pizza become almost as common in Italy as it was in America. In other words, the Northern Italians have America to thank for pizza. And the Americans can thank the Southern Italian immigrants who brought pizza to U.S. shores generations ago. What goes around, comes around.

୪

45/ "It's in the Blood"

One day in Rome, I asked an old man who was sweeping the steps of a church for directions to some place. Instead of giving me the requested information, he smiled delightedly and said:

"*Tu sei italiano!*" (You're Italian!)

"*No, signor, sono americano.*" (No sir, I'm American.) He waived my answer aside, still smiling.

"*Ma, i tuoi genitori sono italiani!*" (But your parents are Italian.)

"*Si, è vero, ma lei come sa?*" (Yes, it's true, but how did you know?)

"*Guarda, gli occhi, la bocca, i capelli, il naso.* (Look, your eyes, mouth, hair, nose.) Then with special emphasis, he added: *Il sangue! Il sangue!* (The blood!).

Yes, the blood, I thought. It's in the blood. It cannot be denied. I suddenly felt quite pleased with myself. I was only eighteen without a firm grip on my self-identity. Now, thanks to this wise old man, I knew who I was: *Sono italiano!* I am Italian! It was most gratifying.

The next day I decided to fully embrace the inescapable truth about my ethnicity. I wore the trimmest, tightest pair of pants I had, which unfortunately were pleated and by Italian standards still rather baggy. My American-style jacket was much too long

145

and loose fitting but I tried to compensate by wearing it the way I had seen Italian actors wear their jackets: draped loosely over their shoulders like capes.

I combed my hair in what I thought better resembled an Italian style. Instead of showing a red pack of Pall Malls sticking out of my jacket pocket, I inserted a greyish pack of *Nazionali*, (back in the days when I smoked). And when I went walking down the street, it was with a slight swagger, the way I had seen actors do in Italian films.

On my first excursion as a real *italiano*, I found myself in the *Foro Romano*, amidst all the haunted ruins of ancient Rome. And lo! Standing there just ten paces ahead was an American. No doubt about it. He wore a grey plaid suit something no Italian would wear, not even to his own funeral. On the American's nose was perched a pair of glasses whose dark horn-rimmed frame was a product almost entirely unknown in Italy. Likewise his heavy, square-toed, black shoes (much like mine) were so different from the finely cut Italian shoes that the men wore. Finally, slung over his shoulder was a bright blue Pan-Am travel bag, and in his hand a tourist book, "Seeing Rome on $5 a Day" or some equivalent. He might just as well have had a neon sign blinking over his head: "HIYA! I'M JOE TOURIST! AN ALL-AMERICAN BOY!"

Here was my perfect prey. I decided to walk up to him and exercise my authentic irrepressible Italian identity. I would ask this foreigner something in Italian, then watch him squirming to make himself understood. What sport.

Scusi, signore, dove sta il vaticano e la chiesa di Santa Maria?" said I. Instead of getting flustered and begging off with "Sorry no speak Italian," he responded:

"Beats me, Jack. I'm an American just like you."

POW! My youthful short-lived pretense exploded in my face like a trick cigar. It was I who suddenly was sputtering. "Oh, uh, I didn't realize you were American. Well, huh, whaddiya know.

Um, I should've noticed what with your travel bag and all."

My newly found identity as a true-blooded *italiano*, an identity so overpoweringly evident to wise old Italian men, suddenly had evaporated, having lasted less than twenty-four hours.

If it was any consolation, years later it became apparent to me that there was no such thing as "Italian blood," no more than is there "American blood" or "French blood" or whatever. I was Italian on both sides of my family which meant to some people that I was a "pure blooded Italian." But this whole idea of blood purity is a ridiculous myth, carried over for too many generations through too many wars, atrocities, and ethnic "cleansings," for centuries making Europe one of the most blood drenched regions of the world. And today, too much of the globe still remains plagued by notions of ethnic supremacy.

Look at a map and see how Italy cuts the heavily trafficked Mediterranean in half. Along with the "indigenous" prehistoric first dwellers, the peoples who inhabited the Italian peninsula were — and are — ancient admixtures of Greeks, Etruscans, Sabines, Ladins, Illyrians, Phoenicians, Cretans, Macedonians, Canaanites, Franks, Goths, Visgoths, Longobards, Normans, Tyrolese, Bavarians, Egyptians, Carthaginians, Arabs, Serbs, Albanians, Spaniards, Portuguese, Austrians, Hungarians, and I'm sure I left out many other groups, ancient and more recent.

All these various peoples in turn are themselves composed of lineages going back into prehistoric times. In other words, *everyone* is a multi-ethnic confection. Nobody, absolutely nobody, has "pure" blood (whatever that is supposed to be) not even the vicious Klansmen and other racist retards in rural America who admittedly might have profited from less inbreeding.

So while I can feel proud of my Italian heritage, I am not making claim to the superiority of my particular gene pool or blood lineage. That fiction would only put me at odds with the rest of the world and deprive me of enjoying the contributions of so many other peoples.

~ Good-bye Columbus ~

One of the historic figures we Italian Americans claim as part of our heritage is Christopher Columbus, unfortunately. Every Columbus Day we march up Fifth Avenue (as proudly as do the Irish on St. Patrick's Day), celebrating Columbus as the "Great Navigator" and "Great Discoverer." One might think that had Columbus not managed to land in the "New World," it would never have been discovered by the Europeans. What a blessing that would have been for the Native Americans. Only in recent times have we recognized that Columbus and his ilk searched not for new worlds but new riches, driven by the *auri sacra fames* (cursed hunger for gold), almost as madly as today's global plutocrats. Some Italian-American authors, teachers, and political activists have joined with Native American groups to publicize how Columbus enslaved and slaughtered the indigenous peoples he encountered, how he set a terrible example that would be followed by slavers and greed-driven bloodletting land grabbers for several centuries afterward. Cristoforo is nobody to be proud of.

ε∂

46/ *Homage to Puglia*

Puglia (pronounced Poolyah) is the region my father's family came from. It is also the name of a restaurant in New York's Little Italy. Located in Lower Manhattan, Little Italy is not to be confused with Italian Harlem (which was in uptown Manhattan). Little Italy was much smaller than Italian Harlem but better known among tourists mostly because of its large concentration of quality restaurants. Today, it still exists, while Italian Harlem has disappeared, now settled by other ethnic groups. But even Little Italy is shrinking away, yielding territory to Chinatown expanding from the south and SoHo expanding from the west.

There was one restaurant (the name of which I cannot recall) just above Little Italy in the southern part of Greenwich Village; it had a *bocce* court right inside the restaurant itself. That area of the "South Village," as it was called, was also an Italian neighborhood as was much of Greenwich Village. But it gave way to gentrification and high rents as the young professionals and gays moved in.

Whenever I see a *bocce* game in progress, I think about an uncle of mine who played *bocce* with his neighbors in Staten Island. I was just an eleven or twelve year old kid spending a couple of weeks out in then-rustic Staten Island with him and my aunt and some cousins. I loved to watch the games that these Italian men pursued with such flair. They would play "boss and underboss" (*capo e sotto capo*). It was the real thing: the court was pressed and smoothed with a heavy earth roller; the *bocce* balls were made of solid wood; and most of the verbal exchanges between the players were in Southern Italian dialect, with a sprinkle of broken English.

After each round of games a bottle of wine was allocated to the victors, to use as they wished. The boss, top winner, made the decisions about distributing the drinks. The underboss could not initiate decisions but he could veto the boss's decisions. Grudges were often acted out. Sometimes a player, forced to go dry by a rival, would retaliate after the next round by denying a drink to that same rival if he had the opportunity. The games and wine allocations were high drama.

All the *bocce* games I have watched since those summer days on Staten Island seem tame and hardly authentic. The *bocce* court in the Greenwich Village restaurant felt disappointingly out of place. I did not enjoy seeing yuppie urbanites awkwardly playing *bocce* a few feet away while I was trying to savor my linguini and clam sauce.

But it is *Puglia Ristorante* that I want to dwell upon. It had no *bocce* court but it had almost everything else. I first chanced upon it while searching for a place that served *capuzella* (in Southern dialect: *gaboozell'*), roasted sheep head or lamb head. The head of the sheep is sawed right down the middle. Each half is a serving in itself, with its crisp meat on the upper skull and jaw, rich tasting brains, a full-length half tongue, and a fatty eyeball. This was back in my untrammeled carnivore days. I have since moved away from meat consumption, but years ago *capuzella* was a savage feast. The meat on the lamb skull was the tastiest and crispiest one could find, especially if well roasted in a brick or stone oven.

The Greeks also ate *capuzella*, though of course they called it something else. I once had *capuzella* at a midtown Greek restaurant. It was served completely boned, with the meat, brain, tongue and eye rearranged on the plate to simulate a sheep head but without the skull itself. For this feat, perhaps, the Greeks deserve some extra credit.

In the late 1950s and 1960s, Puglia Ristorante was the only place I could find outside of East Harlem that served *capuzella.* One could also order *mogliatelli* (sheep's testicles) on a skewer, and *pasta e fagioli* (a soup of macaroni and beans).

Puglia was situated on Hester Street, right across from the old Umberto's Clamhouse, where mobster "Crazy Joey" Gallo was rubbed out by members of the Colombo gang in 1972. The story goes that Gallo was asking for it, traipsing around deep into Colombo territory, and then making the mistake of sitting in Umberto's with his back to the door, allowing the hit men to get the jump on him.

Puglia had other interesting features besides being situated near the site of a mafia hit. It was built in 1919. It had a brick oven that produced grand results with the roasted lamb. When I first discovered Puglia in 1959, it was a completely non-gentrified, unreconstructed restaurant, looking much like a low-grade cafeteria with its long Formica tables, old metal folding chairs, and tiled floor. It was patronized completely by local Italian Americans who stared at you if you were an outsider. The non-Italians had not yet discovered the place. I think it was I who brought the first Jews there, my close friends Howard Kahn and Sherman Miller — who tried to act as Italian as they could at Puglia Ristorante.

Puglia's walls were adorned with amateur paintings that purported to be scenes from the old country. Over the door that led into the kitchen was a plaque with the owner's name, Gregorio Garofalo, and the place of his birth: Gravina di Puglia. I was delighted. "Signor Garofalo!" I called to the aging *padrone*, "My father was born in Gravina, the very same town as you!" I half expected him to leap up and embrace me, fighting back the tears of joy as we both exclaim in Barese dialect *"paesanu meh! paesanu meh!"* ("my countryman!"), maybe followed by a complimentary glass of wine. Instead, he gazed blankly at me and then gave a faint nod of acknowledgment and a grunt. The *padrone* was not impressed.

The one marvelous feature about Puglia Ristorante was the cluster of elderly Italian immigrant men, dressed in trim but well-worn black suits and black hats (white shirts, no ties), nursing glasses of wine or glasses of black coffee. From time to time, one or another of these elders would rise from his seat and sing a Southern Italian ballad from the bottom of his heart and the top of his lungs: *"Vicin' u mare, facim' amore; a cuore cuore..."* in broad Southern dialect vowels, all performed with a bursting sweep of sentimentality yet without the slightest self-consciousness. The other men would listen attentively. After a short interval another would rise and belt out another song of the same vintage.

I was always happy when I went to Puglia Ristorante, drawn back into this precious yesterday. But the years took their toll. By the late 1970s the restaurant was no longer the same. The non-Italians, including Ivy League students, came from all over the city and beyond. The old men had died off, so too the original owner, Garofalo.

As the years went on, the music at Puglia became greatly amplified. A stout lady sang pop American tunes through a microphone—too loudly. In time, the menu grew more elaborate and less authentic, like the music. The singing was now done by local professionals adorned in shiny nightclub attire. Puglia was now the poor man's Las Vegas, pulling in the tourist trade.

The last time I got to Puglia Ristorante was in the autumn of 2010. It was my first visit in over twenty-five years, an accidental one. I had spoken that day at a conference not far from Little Italy. It was Saturday night and the streets of Little Italy were full of strollers. I wandered along with the crowd and to my happy surprise came upon Puglia Ristorante. "Do you still serve *capuzella*?" I asked the man at the door. "No, no," he laughed. "That was a long time ago." I nodded, turned away, and walked off.[32]

I still think of the old men of 1959. I recall their trim black suits and glasses of black coffee and their sad sentimental songs, sung so perfectly without microphones, so possessed of something now

---

[32] Today on Minetta Lane in Greenwich Village there is a restaurant, named Perla, where "obscure peasant delicacies like roasted lamb's head are served as occasional specials," reports *New York* magazine, 30 April 2012.

lost. The thought of them still gives me a tug. I am reminded that yesterday never really returns, no matter how intently we search and wait.

✇

47/ *Coming Home to Both Worlds*

I mourned the loss of the "authentic" Italian-American world of New York, symbolized by the transformation of places like Puglia Ristorante, yet I myself frequently looked beyond the horizon. In other words, I did not want outsiders intruding upon my ethnic enclosure, but I certainly wanted to go romping into their far-off gardens and pathways.

Often during my childhood I would wonder about the world beyond East Harlem, about the strange inhabitants of downtown, East Side Manhattan, tall, pink-faced, Anglo-Protestants who pronounced all their r's, patronized the Broadway theater, and traveled to Europe for purposes other than to locate lost relatives. I would think of other unexplored worlds with anticipation. This "intoxication of experiences yet to come" left me with the keen feeling that East Harlem was not my final destination in life.

I was not the only one preparing to pull up stakes and wander off to new terrain. Most of the Italians, including all my relatives, abandoned East Harlem by the late 1950s, moving to second settlement areas, leaving the old neighborhood to growing numbers of Puerto Rican and other Latino immigrants. The money the Italians had saved during the war years and post-war "prosperity" became the down-payment passage to the mass-produced housing tracts of Long Island, Staten Island, Westchester County, and New Jersey, where as proud homeowners they could live a life that approximated the middle-class suburban one they saw in the movies.

But the new lifestyle had a downside to it. One uncle, who used to have huge parties for friends and relatives in his home on

Third Avenue, complete with mandolins and accordions, popular songs and operatic arias—drawn from the amateur talents of the guests themselves—now discovered that no one came to visit him, marooned as he now was on the outer edge of Queens. An aunt of mine, who had lived all her life within shouting distance of at least two of her four sisters, tearfully told my mother how lonely she was in Staten Island, "out in the sticks."

In time, I went off to graduate school and saw far less of my extended family, as they did of each other. Years later, in 1968, I got a call from my Cousin Anthony asking me to attend a family reunion (my mother's side of the family). As Anthony put it, "It seems nowadays we only get together for weddings and funerals. And lately, there have not been enough weddings and too many funerals."

So here it was, a family reunion. It took place in his home in Queens, attended by a crowd of cousins and their fourth-generation children, the latter being youngsters whom I was meeting for the first time and for whom East Harlem was nothing more than a geographical expression, if even that.

Time had brought its changes. The women wore coiffures and stylish clothes, and the men looked heavier. There was much talk about recent vacations and a slide show of Cousin Anthony's travels to Europe, also a fine buffet of Italian foods that made the slide show worth sitting through. And there were a lot of invitations to "come visit us."

Much to my disappointment, the older surviving aunts and uncles had decided to stay away because this was an affair for the younger people, an act of age segregation that would have been unthinkable in earlier times. In all, we spent a pleasant evening joking and catching up on things. It was decided we should get together more often. But we never did have another reunion.

In the late 1970s I began to have a recurring dream, every few months or so. Unlike the recurring dreams portrayed in movies (in which the exact same footage is run and rerun) the particulars and fixtures of each dream in real life—or real sleep—differ, but the underlying theme is the same.

In each dream, I found myself living in a fashionable New York apartment; sometimes it had spiral stairwells and bare brick walls and sometimes lavish wood paneling and fireplaces, but it always turned out to be an upscale renovation of my parents' simple apartment at 304 East 118th Street, the old brownstone in East Harlem where I had spent much of my early life.

We might think of recurring dreams as nightmarish, but these dreams of mine were accompanied by sensations of relief and yearning. The life past was being recaptured and renovated by the life now accomplished. The slum was being gentrified. The working-class Italian youth and the professional-class American academic were to live together under the same roof.

I had come home to two worlds apart. Never quite at home in either one, I would now have the best of both. Once I understood the message, the dreams stopped.

~ The End ~

ABOUT THE AUTHOR

Michael Parenti was born and raised in an Italian-American working class family in New York City. After high school he worked for some years then returned to school and eventually earned an M.A. from Brown University and a Ph.D. in political science from Yale University. His twenty-five books include *The Face of Imperialism* (2011); *God and His Demons* (2010); *Contrary Notions: The Michael Parenti Reader* (2007); *The Assassination of Julius Caesar* (2003); and *Democracy for the Few, 9th edition* (2010).

Portions of his writings have been translated into some twenty languages. Books and articles of his have been used extensively in college courses and also by lay readers. Hundreds of his articles have been published in scholarly journals, popular magazines and newspapers, books of collected readings, and online publications.

Dr. Parenti lectures frequently across North America and abroad. Tapes of his various talks and interviews have played widely on community radio stations, public access television, and the internet.

His work covers a wide range of subjects, including politics, history, empire, wealth, class power, culture, ideology, media, environment, gender, and ethnic life. Dr. Parenti has won awards from various academic and community organizations. For more information, visit his website: www.MichaelParenti.org.

VIA FOLIOS
A refereed book series dedicated to the culture of Italians and Italian Americans.

Bordighera Press is an imprint of Bordighera, Incorporated, an independently owned not-for-profit scholarly organization that has no legal affiliation with the University of Central Florida or with The John D. Calandra Italian American Institute, Queens College/CUNY.

CPSIA information can be obtained
at www.ICGtesting.com
Printed in the USA
FSOW01n1406050914
3081FS